CHAKRA HEALING

*Techniques to Activate, Unblock, and Balance
Chakras for your full-body Energy Cleanse*

Asana Swami & Richard Reikivic

youbooks editions

Table of Contents

Download the Audio Book Version of This Book for FREE

If you love listening to audiobooks on the go, I have great news for you. You can download the audiobook version of this book for **FREE** just by signing up for a **FREE** 30-day Audible trial! See below for more details!

Audible Trial Benefits

As an audible customer, you will receive the below benefits with your 30-day free trial:

- FREE audible book copy of this book
- After the trial, you will get 1 credit each month to use on any audiobook
- Your credits automatically roll over to the next month if you don't use them
- Choose from Audible's 200,000 + titles
- Listen anywhere with the Audible app across multiple devices
- Make easy, no-hassle exchanges of any audiobook you don't love
- Keep your audiobooks forever, even if you cancel your membership.

SCAN THE QR CODE AND GET YOUR FREE AUDIBLE BOOK

FOR AUDIBLE US

FOR AUDIBLE UK

FOR AUDIBLE FR

FOR AUDIBLE DE

audible

an amazon company

FREE BOOKS SENT WEEKLY

JOIN YOUBOOKS EDITIONS

READERS BOOKCLUB

and

get exclusive access to the latest kindle e-book

FIND YOUR BONUS
AT THE END OF THE BOOK

Introduction

Your third eye is your ability to see potential or what might be. You likely do not realize that you use your third eye often. You utilized your third eye the last time you had a hunch and acted on it. It is sometimes referred to as the sixth sense because it can aid you in making decisions. You can refine your third eye to improve its accuracy so that you can have more excellent guidance in all areas of your life.

Opening your third eye is the first step in taking a more significant advantage. However, it is a process; you must be ready to open it to ensure success. The process involves trial and error, and you must exercise patience.

To the naked eye, the third eye is not visible. However, it is considered to be located between both of your eyebrows on your forehead. It is the central source of your imagination, intuition, and inner wisdom. Because of this, it is often described as an energetic eye instead of a physical one.

The spot where the third eye is located connects to the pineal gland in the body. This gland is located in the brain, a type of endocrine gland. Physically, it is responsible for the production of melatonin, a kind of hormone in the body associated with seasonal and sleep patterns. Once you activate this gland, it causes your third eye to open.

Several strategies may aid you in opening your third eye. Consider the following techniques when you are ready to awaken your third eye:

Cultivate silence: The silence of the mind should be fostered, and one of the most effective ways to do this is with meditation. To take full advantage of the messages that your third eye provides, you have to be able to hear its whisper. With a calm and quiet mind, this is possible. A busy reason is far more vulnerable to missing critical messages.

Hone your intuition: The center of your vision, higher wisdom, and insight is your third eye. This is also where you will find higher levels of intuition and perception. Being curious is one way to encourage your third eye to open. You become more confident in utilizing your third eye as you learn more.

Nurture your creativity: Let your imagination run wild when you can. You can also focus your creativity on specific activities at a time. Learning how to do a new type of art is easy to accomplish. You do not have to be perfect or highly skilled to take advantage of this. You will also have to work on your rational mind. Loosen it, and do not be afraid to think about things that are not entirely based on logic. Read fairytales or legends like Bigfoot to get outside of the truth and consider other possibilities.

Ground yourself: Your third eye requires a grounded body and mind to be the most beneficial. You can better interpret the extrasensory perceptions when you create a reliable foundation for them. This also increases your overall clarity about different areas of your life. Your body has a constant stream of energy running throughout it. You want to keep the channels open so that the point can expand and aid you in higher levels of perception. This also alleviates confusion and disorientation when the third eye opens.

Chapter 1.   What Are Chakras

Chakras are subtle energy centers located in places of nerve plexuses. Chakra in Sanskrit means "wheel." There are seven main chakras in our subtle body, each corresponding to a stage of evolution. Each chakra is responsible for embodying certain spiritual qualities that most people are in an unmanifest state.

Chakras are the most well-known elements of the subtle body theory. Many authors interested in yoga, Tibetan Buddhism, Theosophy, and parapsychological research have described the chakras and their comments. Although the seven stages of samadhi are already mentioned in classical yogic sutras, the development of chakras probably began only with the advent of tantric practices.

Often trembling, twitching, twisting, or vibration occurs in the areas of the chakras in people during a massage session or during emotional or physical stress. In these places, a block does not allow energy to move uniformly throughout the body. Blocks may be created by unresolved issues or mental problems associated with chakras. This is related to physical disorders in the functioning of the organs of the human body since most of the chakras control the work of specific organs.

Another phenomenon that can be correlated with the action of the energy of the chakras is the spontaneous occurrence of unique images, sounds, and symbols, which in tantric cosmology are considered inherent in all chakras. Their appearance during crisis conditions can give information related to those issues that need to be resolved or indicate the area of the body, focusing on which will bring the most significant effect. For these reasons, it is helpful to have an idea of the chakra system, which is outlined here - in general terms.

Chakras are called such objects as neurohormonal mechanisms of controlling zones of the body; multidimensional passages through which creative forces flow between three bodies; centers of the body's energy system; energy funnels; intermediaries that transfer energy from one dimension to another; "interdimensional transforming systems that can be controlled by thought and which turn matter into energy" (Joy); centers of subtle forces, cosmic consciousness and prana generation.

According to Goswami, the Bindu of the chakras in the sphere of pranic energy play the same role as atoms in the material sphere. He said: "A moving or active pranic force concentrates and gathers to form petals of Bindu at various points in the body, which in yoga are called chakras, or lotuses. This formation begins with the Sahasrara chakra and continues with the lower chakras with how human consciousness is formed and his material body. All this is invisible to the naked eye. The chakras function on a supermaterial level. "

Usually, the chakras are the connecting link between all types of activities of the causal, subtle, and gross bodies. From them come the vritti (waves of thoughts), as well as other energies that are distributed throughout the body. Therefore, each of them is attributed to certain emotions and properties. Let's take the chakras as the leading converters and energy transmitters between bodies. It will become clear that increasing the tension of consciousness and energy is a powerful additional load on the chakra system. Often, chakras are described as lotuses moving from bottom to top with energy rising through them.

The chakras contain all the untangled nodes and problems of a person's personal and emotional life. During spiritual transformation, they can integrate forms of consciousness that are more characteristic of a unifying function and less ego-oriented.

There are seven main chakras and 43 less critical, attributed to many properties in different texts. It is believed that prana alternately dominates in other chakras according to a sixty-minute rhythm throughout the day. Several types of symbols are associated with each of the main chakras. The latter include an animal personifying the subtle forces that control the chakra; God, which denotes one of the forces of divine manifestation; a goddess, who indicates the type of energy placed at this point. Other symbols represent the dominant element and one of the five senses associated with this chakra. Meditation on each chakra awakens the goddess's power there, opening up unique divine opportunities for man. Lotus petals represent various qualities, emotional tendencies, and possibilities.

The Chakra System

ROOT CHAKRA   SACRAL CHAKRA   SOLAR PLEXUS CHAKRA   HEART CHAKRA   THROAT CHAKRA   THIRD EYE CHAKRA   CROWN CHAKRA

The First Chakra - Muladhara Chakra

Located almost at the end of the spine and touching the anus and testicles or cervix, this chakra is designated as the four-petalled lotus, whose petals represent ultimate happiness, innate bliss, the bliss of unity, and bliss of courage and strength. She is considered a reflection of the crown chakra on the physical level; therefore, her petals are blissful. The nature of this chakra is identical to Brahman, the creative principle of the universe. We can assume that it preserves the material form of the body and that its underlying history and the potential of human evolution are hidden.

MULADHARA
Sanskrit: मूलाधार
ROOT CHAKRA

This is the foundation and support of the body, and its safety and self-preservation depend on its normal functioning. This chakra corresponds to the element earth, orange-red color, and sense of smell. An elephant with a black stripe around the neck is its symbol and represents earthly qualities: strength, firmness, stability, and support; these qualities are represented by the yellow square inscribed in the circle of yantra or mandala depicting this chakra. It also has a triangle called Tripura, representing will, knowledge, and action.

Muladhara affects the rectum, kidneys, sperm accumulation, and genitals, as well as bones, skin, muscles, nerves, and hair. It is associated with physiological disorders such as hemorrhoids, constipation, sciatica, and prostate diseases. It is related to a sense of smell, and its vibration causes the expansion or contraction of the lungs.

Mishra writes that through pratyahara (distraction of the senses), anger, lust, and greed are curbed on this chakra. Longing and depression are also considered symptoms of an imbalance in them.

Meditation on this chakra establishes control over attachments to luxury, lies, pride, envy, and narcissism. Pandit said that the Muladhara controls physical or subconscious movements or impulses. In the yantra (the symbolic image of the chakra), a blood-red triangle of fire inflates the kandarpa Vayu, the cause of sexual arousal, which is essential for reproducing the human race. Motoyama wrote that when this chakra awakens, it releases suppressed emotions explosively, leading to extreme irritability and psychological instability in a person, a violation of sleep patterns, and excitability.

Meditation on the God of this chakra, Mahadeva, who sits with his face, turned back, cleanses from sins. Brahma, the God of absolute creative power, also gives this chakra to the goddess Dakini Shakti, the energy of creation. If you repeat the mul mantra while maintaining the serenity of the mind and devotion and focusing on this chakra, you can awaken her goddess. In yoga cosmology, strictly under this chakra is the Kundalini energy, curled up in three and a half turns. Yogis believe that this is where the confluence of Sushumna (Nadi, carrying the stream of life), Vajra Nadi (Nadi bringing the electric stream), and Brahma Nadi (sound stream or stream of spirit) merge.

The Second Chakra - Svadhishthana Chakra

Located slightly above the Muladhara at the base of the penis or in the center of the lower back, this chakra is associated with the conquest of water; its symbols are the crescent and the God Vishnu, nourishing the principle of the universe. Its color is usually considered red or scarlet and sometimes - white. Ragini Shakti, a dark blue goddess with three red eyes and four hands, carries the energy of this chakra from whose nose blood flows. She holds a trident, a lotus, a drum, and a chisel in her hands. A light gray or green sea monster resembling a crocodile is an animal symbol of the chakra; it personifies dominance over the sea and indicates a connection with the unconscious. By meditating on this chakra, a person defeats the elements.

She has six petals, representing the mental qualities of neglect, numbness, credulity, suspicion, desire for destruction, cruelty, and six nerves associated with the colon, rectum, kidneys, bladder, genitals, etc., and testicles. This chakra promotes the circulation of liquid substances in the body, their conservation, and nutrition; it is also considered a center of the heterosexual orientation of a person.

Mishra wrote that this chakra controls, controls, and nourishes the feet. By focusing on it, a person feels a magnetic pulsation, circulation, and vibration and can get rid of all the unpleasant sensations, pains, and illnesses in his legs. Other conditions associated with this chakra include sexual problems, diabetes, and kidney and bladder diseases. People are freed from egoistic feelings, tiny impulses, and desires by meditating on them. The stability and serenity of the mind develop. The normal functioning of the Svadhishthana is associated with a sense of self-confidence and well-being and the frustrations in her work, disappointment, addiction, and anxiety. This chakra is also associated with a sense of taste and language. According to some tantras, to master it, a person must master the language.

The Third Chakra - Manipura Chakra

Located above Svadvishthana opposite the navel, Manipura is associated with Rudra, a god who distributes goods and creates fear, personifying the destructive principle of the universe (the world of the mind). The goddess Lakini Shakti, dressed in yellow clothes, is called the benefactress of the universe, and one of the texts describes that she loves animal meat, her chest is covered with blood, and fat is dripping from her lips. The animal symbol is a ram, sacrificed animal, which personifies the need to sacrifice addictions, impulsive urges, and other strong emotions.

Concentration over Manipura brings comprehension of feces or eternal time. Perhaps this level of openness can be associated with returning memories of other lives or states that take people beyond the boundaries of consciousness created by time. This chakra is also related to heat control and directs the Agni, the fiery principle, which controls the creature's uncontrolled movements and digestive system. Manipura governs the internal organs of the abdomen, in particular, the functioning of the stomach, liver, and large intestine, and is associated with a section of the central nervous system located above the lumbar region. Some say that focusing on this center can cure diseases of the abdominal organs, especially if you meditate on its red color.

Ten petals that carry the qualities of shame, betrayal, envy, desire, drowsiness, despondency, vainness, delusion, disgust, and fear make up this chakra. However, according to one of the tantric texts, when a yogi meditates on this chakra and pronounces a mul mantra, he is always in a good mood, and illnesses cannot penetrate their body. Such a yogi can enter into the bodies of others and see Siddhas (saints and teachers of yoga), can, at a glance, determine the qualities of material objects, and see things underground. It is clear why this chakra is so often associated with gaining power and finding a good place in the world. It is also challenging that focuses on some Zen meditations. This concentration gives rise to a sense of stability and resilience in the being,

The opening of this chakra requires the participation of the eyes and such control over their movements so that they do not, for a moment, come off the center between the eyebrows.

The Fourth Chakra - Anahata Chakra

The heart chakra location is usually opposite the centerline running between the nipples. Still, sometimes it is moved slightly to the right of the sternum, although not directly above the heart. It is associated with the conquest of air, nature, and nada, the sound of cosmic consciousness. By meditating on this center, you can feel how the energy flows throughout the entire nervous system as if it is filled with magnetism. Many traditions of spiritual development emphasize the importance of the heart chakra as the chakra that needs to be awakened in the first place to experience a spiritual awakening since it is here that the energies of the lower and upper levels of consciousness merge, which symbolize two intersecting triangles. In addition, Anahata, combining the powers of different chakras, also connects the left and right sides of the body, yin and yang qualities.

Isha is the God of this chakra; he sits on a black antelope or gazelle, which symbolizes speed and ease of air. Isha is the supreme God, endowed with full yogic power, omniscient, and omnipresent. It is white and symbolizes purity; it has three eyes; the third represents knowledge of samadhi. When its form arises during meditation, fears disappear, and concentration intensifies.

The yantra images of the heart chakra include intersecting triangles, inside which are a bright golden creature and Kakini Shakti, the lightning-colored goddess who radiates light and joy. Kakini is called the keeper of Anahata's doors and meditates on it; a person learns to stabilize prana and remove obstacles on the way to Isha. When the goddess is red, her power controls pranic energy; she is white and is Isha's consciousness.

The twelve scarlet petals associated with Anahata represent waiting, excitement, diligence, affection, hypocrisy, weakness, selfishness, separation, greed, fraud, indecision, and regret. Meditation on this chakra brings possession of sound. If you say the mul mantra during meditation, you are more prepared to understand God, as a person gains control over his feelings, mainly by reducing the sense of touch.

Then, as they say, not a single desire will remain unfulfilled - a person will forever plunge into a state of bliss.

Suppose you look from a different point of view. In that case, we can assume that freed from attachment to all "heart" desires (as evidenced by the qualities embodied in the petals), a person gains the ability to distract the senses from all worldly things and thus acquire a state of bliss first for short periods and then forever.

The qualities of compassion, acceptance, and unconditional love are signs of the balanced functioning of this chakra. Indifference, passivity, and sadness are signs of an imbalance — some authors associate arthritis and respiratory problems with cardiac chakra, cardiovascular disease, and hypertension.

The opening of this chakra is considered feasible with the help of the skin; that is, you need to surpass the sense of touch, which is done by achieving control over sensory perception through kumbhaka (breath-holding). A common way to discover the energy of Anahata is a meditation on it with the simultaneous presentation of light or breathing in and breathing out air from it.

The Fifth Chakra - Vishuddha Chakra

Located in the throat is the vishuddhi lotus - gray or silver (and sometimes smoky purple) and has sixteen petals. They contain seven musical notes, poison and nectar, and seven "invocations," which are used to protect against demons, during sacrifices, to sacred light lights, to give determination, to bless and glorify. Here begin the priestly or occult powers associated with the forces of projection or expression. This chakra is also related to conquering the etheric state of matter (space). This chakra is usually associated with creative activity and inspiration, as well as receiving moral instruction, especially when in contact with an inexhaustible source of "grace." A person begins to feel that the inner giver and taker are the same.

The God of this chakra is Shiva in a half-male, half-female form (Ardhanarishvara); he sits on a white elephant and the four-armed yellow Shakini Shakti (goddess). He owns a variety of knowledge. She rules in the kingdom of the moon over little secrets.

Vishuddha controls both hands and is the center of pratyahara, or distraction of the senses. When a person focuses attention here, he loses sensitivity to heat, cold, pain, pressure, touch, and temperature. Tantras say that the instruments of this chakra are ears; they are used so that the world's noise does not distract, and only one sound is heard: either nada (the sound of Ohms is less intense) or the name of God. Meditation on this chakra leads one to the threshold of great liberation.

The Sixth Chakra - Ajna Chakra

Ajna is located above the nose between the eyebrows and is the source of two nerve flows, one passing through the eyes and the other through the midbrain. There are three main Nadi (Sushumna, Ida, and Pingala). The ability to create and achieve is generated by mental waves emanating from this point. This chakra controls the will and knowledge's inner vision and dynamic activity. This "third eye" is associated with light, internal knowledge, intuition, and mediumistic abilities in many cultures. The discovery of these abilities involves the integration of both intellectual and emotional poles.

The goddess of Ajna is the six-faced and six-armed Hakini Shakti; she personifies the five principles concentrated in the lower chakras and the gifts of the Ajna chakra. When its color is described as red, the knowledge of Kundalini is fully awakened; when she is white, she represents a state of rest; when it is dark blue, it is on the verge of transitioning into a shapeless form. When seen in a combination of white, red, and black colors, she shows a mixture of three gunas: sattva (harmonious consciousness), rajas (activity), and tamas (inertia).

Meditation at this center brings visions of the highest truth, yogic powers, liberation from all Sanskars, and ultimately wisdom, higher knowledge. This is the center of individual consciousness, expanding to universal through pratyahara. Ajna is often referred to as guiding all other chakras, and some yogis advise concentrating only on it, or first of all, before awakening energies in other centers. Thus, the development of the qualities inherent in all previous chakras can be influenced so that the student can achieve a nondual consciousness. It is believed that it is impossible to master the lower chakras fully before Ajna is awakened.

The Seventh Chakra - Sahasrara Chakra

According to some texts, Sahasrara is located at the top of the head in the brain; others believe that it is above the physical body and is identical to Parabrahma, the supreme creator. Her lotus has a thousand petals, five of which represent all the letters of the Sanskrit alphabet. Samadhi, felt through this chakra, is a complete merger with existence without the limits of ego-consciousness in the body. (Although there are yoga systems in which other levels of chakras are indicated, extending further beyond the physical body and to this first level of higher consciousness.)

SAHASRARA
Sanskrit: सहस्रार
CROWN CHAKRA

Parabrahma governs this center, symbolized by the triangle of consciousness, called Vija- another name for the divine essence of sat-chit-ananda. It represents overcoming obstacles and merging with emptiness or the Upper Light outside the form, a state that a person cannot describe, according to most yogic sacred books and the saying of the saints.

Meditating here, according to Bose and Haldor, a person crosses the boundaries of creation, preservation, and destruction and can taste the sweet nectar (amrita) flowing in a continuous stream from Sahasrara. A person is freed, all Sanskars are destroyed, and he is not subject to either birth or death. At this stage of awakening, individual identification disappears forever, and a person is identified with a higher consciousness. (It is important to remember that when yogis talk about the state of immortality, they usually do not mean that a person will never leave the body, but rather imply that conscious fusion with the infinite is achieved forever and will not be destroyed with the death of the body).

Chakra Healing

Chapter 2.   Opening Your Third Eye

The third eye is home to a person's sixth sense. When fully open and balanced, you become more intuitive and attain higher wisdom. It is not easy to open the third eye chakra, and most people find it challenging.

Prepare yourself first by doing the following steps:

1. Nurture silence. Find ways that will help you in fostering the stillness of the mind. You can try focusing on art or sport, being one with nature, or meditating. Your mind must remain calm so it won't miss any message from the other realm.

2. Develop your intuition. You have to practice intuitive techniques to make understanding the messages and visions you'll be getting easier. Have fun in the process, and do not feel burdened with the tasks involved. Learn how to read tarot cards and horoscopes and familiarize themselves with the meanings of dreams.

3. Let your creativity flow. You have to find ways to loosen your rational mind. Get inspired to try out new hobbies, crafts, and arts. You don't have to be perfect and don't need to pressure yourself to always come up with something. You must enjoy the process and let your imagination take you wherever it leads you. The practice will calm your mind, increasing your third eye's capacity to unfold and improve.

4. Be grounded all the time. This critical foundation will allow you to understand your extrasensory perceptions clearly. If you are not grounded, you might feel confused and disturbed by the images and thoughts coming to you. It helps in opening the subtle channels of perception. This will avoid the common adverse effects of having an open third eye.

Once you have prepared yourself for what is about to happen, you can perform simple but effective exercises to support the opening of your sixth chakra. Here are some of the activities that will help in boosting your intuitive energy center:

- Reflect and rest under the moonlight. The light coming from the moon is similar to the light of your intuitive center.

- The primary function of your third eye is intuition, so always find ways to exercise this ability.

- Strengthening the energy from the chakras helps unlock the powers of your third eye and keep it balanced, such as the first and throat chakras.

- Embrace silence because this is your gate to hear the whisper of the third eye's wisdom.

- Contemplate and meditate.

- Cultivate your psychic abilities.

- Learn how to work with spirit guides.

- Always be curious about everything around you, including symbols and their meanings.

The Role of the Pineal Gland in Awakening the Third Eye

The position of the third eye is associated with both the pineal and pituitary glands. The pituitary gland is the human body's master gland because it controls other glands and produces hormones. On the other hand, the pineal gland is situated at the same level as the eyes and right at the brain's center. It is found behind and above the pituitary gland.

Modern metaphysics and yogic traditions view the pineal gland as the seat of the soul and source of psychic powers, extrasensory perception, and mystical experiences. The gland's functions are similar to the cycles of light and darkness.

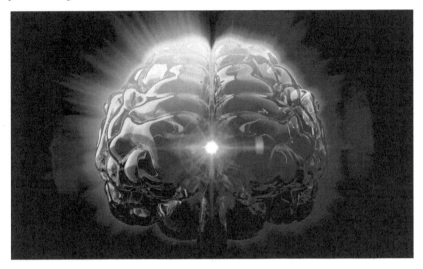

Here are the exercises that you must do to boost the ability of the pineal gland to awaken your third eye:

- Meditate. It kindles the part of the brain that boosts the pineal gland and helps keep the balance of your nervous system.

- Step outside and bask in the glory of the sunshine.

- Find some time to spend in complete darkness. It stimulates the production of the pineal gland's hormones and keeps it active and healthy.

- Eat supplements and foods that help in keeping the pineal gland healthy.

The pineal gland gets more blood flow than any other organ in the body and is surrounded by highly charged cerebrospinal fluid. It is also a rich source of melatonin and contains the highest concentration of energy.

Melatonin is a known antioxidant and anti-stress, and anti-aging agent. It affects a person's quality and length of sleep, circadian rhythms, immune function, and mood. Light and darkness affect the pineal gland's production of melatonin. Light prevents the show, and it is activated by darkness.

Once melatonin is released into the system, it circulates to the brain through the pineal gland's blood before it goes into the blood vessels to get distributed throughout the body.

Keeping the pineal gland healthy and activated is essential since it has spiritual connections. Ancient Egyptians preserved this tiny pinecone-shaped gland separately during the mummification process. It is also an artifact in many ancient traditions wherein it has been linked with immortality and enlightenment. Its shape symbolizes the perfect sequence of Fibonacci as it represents creation and growth.

This gland is also the key to opening the third eye. Here are some of the basic techniques that you can follow to activate the pineal gland:

1. Tapping. Gently tap your forehead where the third eye chakra is situated. The vibration activates the pineal gland, stimulates the pituitary gland, and awakens the hypothalamus.

2. Breathing. Proper breathing increases the potency of cerebrospinal fluid or CSF. Learn the different breathing practices that boost the flow of CSF.

3. Squeezing. The pituitary gland is activated when you squeeze your eyes. To stimulate cranial pumps and neck, move your jaw by sucking your cheeks. As the perineum and anal sphincter contract, vibrations are sent to the muscles surrounding the pelvic floor. The beat will then move up the spine to the occiput before moving to the central part of the head to activate both the pituitary and pineal glands.

4. Toning. Also referred to as chanting, it energizes the CSF and activates the pineal and other glands in the process.

5. Smiling and laughing. Your heart and crown open up when you smile. As a result, more light can penetrate, increasing the vibration of the organs. Smiling and laughing also help your body relax and reduce stress, allowing a good flow of chi or energy throughout the body. Relaxation also boosts blood flow, which helps in activating the pineal gland. Laughing is generally beneficial to health as it triggers the release of the hormones that help promote feelings of well-being, known as endorphins.

6. Spending time in darkness. Darkness boosts melatonin production. Once released, it activates the pineal gland and stimulates the production of proline and DMT.

7. Pressing. Feel the roof of your mouth and press your tongue in it. The simple task activates the pituitary gland and, in the process, activates the pineal gland and hypothalamus through chemical and physical connections.

8. Focus. Bring your attention to the location of whatever you want to activate, and your energy will flow in that direction.

9. Spiraling movements. These movements include spinning the Tai Chi symbol or pakua to form an electromagnetic field and bring more energy to the CSF. It will then enhance the heart field's power and activate the pineal gland.

Activating the Third Eye Chakra

When the third eye is open and balanced, your focus and concentration improve, and you become more intuitive and reliant. Here are some practices to follow to hone such skills by activating the third eye chakra:

1. Practice mindful breathing. It calms the mind, opens and cleanses the third eye, and helps balance the chakra system.

2. Add the colors representing the third eye chakra to your surroundings. You can wear clothes with the hues of the color indigo or fill your office or home with accents in colors of the same shades.

3. Add fruits and vegetables in purple and natural blue hues. You can eat the fruits fresh or turn them into a beverage.

4. Always find time to practice third eye meditation. Engage your third eye whenever you have time. This can quickly be done through meditation and visualization. Sit somewhere quiet, close your eyes, and visualize purple or blue ball energy in the location of your third eye. Hold that image as much as you can by concentrating. The activity will open up the energy center and help heal and balance the chakra.

5. Keep a dream journal. You have to practice remembering your dreams and learning about their meanings.

6. Use essential oils with mild fragrances to open, cleanse, and balance the chakras. You can use one or a combination of any of the following oils to heal and activate your third eye chakra:

- Nutmeg

- Grapefruit

- Roman or German Chamomile

- Myrrh

- Sandalwood

Third Eye Chakra Stones

You can use various gemstones, crystals, and healing stones to open, balance, and heal your chakra system. These healing stones have different properties and unique vibrational energy frequencies. Here are some of the crystals and stones that you can use, including their purpose and meaning:

1. Black Obsidian. This semi-precious stone comes in color black. It gets rid of chakra blockages and negativity. It also helps in enhancing your emotional control. The stone is used for balance and stimulation.

2. Purple Fluorite. This semi-precious stone boosts focus and mental clarity. It also promotes intuition and dispels negativity. The stone is used for balance and stimulation.

3. Moldavite. This semi-precious stone comes in the color dark green. It enhances dreams and makes it easier for you to recall them. It can restore the balance of the whole chakra system. It is also used in clearing negativity, restoring balance, stimulating, and cleansing.

4. Amethyst. The color of this precious stone varies from light to dark shades of purple. It is considered a healing stone that protects you from harm, heals, and offers wisdom. It is also used to restore balance, stimulate, and open your third eye.

Chapter 3.   Chakra Meditation

Maybe you consider reflection a demonstration of sitting leg over leg and murmuring to oneself. This isn't all that contemplation is about. You will discover a wide range of many contemplation types that help you unwind and diminish pressure. Chakra is a particular type of reflection that starts from Hindu convictions. Today, the specialty of chakra reflection has spread to each edge of the globe.

Chakra Meditation is a type of reflection comprising many unwinding procedures that bring parity, unwinding, and prosperity to the chakras. "Chakra" is an old Sanskrit word that implies a vortex or wheel that can be followed back to India.

Chakras are the human body's seven primary vitality focuses, with everyone relating to singular organs that administer our particular body parts and different regions of the mind. They are situated alongside a hormonal organ along the human spinal segment.

Chakras can wind up blocked, and if even one of the 7 Chakras ends up blocked, it sets us up for physical and passionate issues nobody needs.

How Do Chakra Meditation Techniques Work?

Our fantastic and puzzling universe circulates its astonishing life-power vitality to the earth and our organs and organs situated throughout the body and circulatory system. This life-power vitality is key vital to acquiring ideal prosperity and well-being. It's accepted that since the chakras are interrelated, they intently influence each other by attempting to accomplish the perfect degree of equalization.

Make Each Cell in Your Body Stir and Celebrate!

A large portion of us has vigorous squares and awkward nature just as vitality attacking propensities that keep us from getting to our full essentialness, which makes us feel depleted, dispersed, dull, and even sick.

The Benefits of Meditation

If new to meditation, questions concerning a capacity to do it can surface, bringing up issues like "How would I consider nothing?" or considerations like "I can't do that." It can appear odd to attempt to discharge ourselves from the pending negative issues in life by what may appear to be a straightforward demonstration of sitting idle, particularly when compelling, passionate battles can mist our psyche.

It very well may be hard to clear your head when such a significant amount of weight from the outside world pulls you down. Yet, it is significantly progressively fundamental during these unpleasant stages throughout everyday life. When I began contemplating, another point of view on life conquered me. These are only a few proposals from an energetic tenderfoot that may enable somebody to start a remunerating routine regarding reflection and mindfulness.

One practice that has helped me keep my brain in the ideal spot when reflecting is checking through breaths. As I breathe in, I fit until I've finished living in, by and large, around eight for me, yet it can be anything depending upon how quick or moderate your tally. I tally to a similar number as I breathe out, arriving at eight when I've finished my breath out. Rehashing this procedure, I add to eight, breathing in through my nose, and after that, considering to eight, I breathe out through my mouth.

Cool air in/warm let some circulation into. I have likewise thought it was gainful to focus on my breaths as calm, positive vitality filling my lungs and leaving as friendly, negative vitality that has been stockpiled inside being discharged. Every breath is imagined, envisioning the positive, new cloud streaming through my nose and pushing the negative, stale cloud out as I breathe through my mouth.

Concentrate on a solitary item. Another training that can encourage contemplation is to concentrate on a solitary article. The item can be anything. I usually picture alone; the light lit in a dim life with nothing else around. I watch it glint as contemplations go through my brain, mindful of them, however giving no consideration. As I get it, this sort of contemplation has been utilized to help recuperate explicit pieces of the body.

Use sound for ruminating. A bit much, yet something that has helped me out a lot, playing a sound can help with "timing" sessions, liberating me from considering to what extent I've been thinking. The utilization of sound can get you more profound and quicker. However, I have a houseful with five youngsters, so putting on earphones and covering up for twenty minutes is, once in a while, the main route for me to work on contemplating.

Practice each day. The increasingly more you accomplish something, the simpler and simpler it gets. This remains constant for reflection, as well. Doing it builds up a sound propensity for taking a refreshing break and recognizing the present, excessively effectively overlooked with our bustling timetables in this day and age. Practice each day and see what opens up for you.

I'm still new to the act of reflection, so I comprehend the anxiety with newness. Be that as it may, I can't overlook the advantages of thinking as they are read and experienced for myself, further supporting the idea that we are in charge of our condition. Also, as I proceed with my routine of contemplation, I am charmingly astonished by the positive vitality I feel when setting aside the effort to find myself.

The Health Benefits of Energy Healing

It's incredibly fascinating to take note that dependent on a distributed American Heart Association's examination in November of 2012 about the effect of pressure decrease projects utilizing reflection; the discoveries demonstrated that contemplation extraordinarily lessens stroke, cardiovascular failure, passing, outrage levels, and the dangers related with coronary supply route illness.

The aftereffects of the program are exceptionally significant with the members who contemplated twice daily for 20 minutes daily. They could diminish coronary episodes and stroke hazards by 48 percent. Furthermore, they likewise declined their annoyance levels. It's intriguing to note that the more continuous the contemplation sessions, the higher the positive medical advantages for the members.

Adapting to consistent outrage is very damaging to the brain and body. There are sure things that one should relinquish or leave without a desire for change. To refer to one model, poisonous connections are not fatal; they hinder recuperating.

Chakra Meditation Music and Chakra Colors to Meditate

Music is another control that is additionally utilized in adjusting the chakras. Notwithstanding the music, the chief has included numerous wonderful and brilliant pictures. These chakra vitality hues are likewise a significant mending segment.

Chakra hues incorporate green, identifying with the substance and discharging genuinely stifled injury. Another powerful shading is indigo for the third eye, encouraging us to see flawlessness. Blue is likewise utilized with throat chakra reflection and the declaration of truth through discourse.

Different methods to help reflection incorporate guided symbolism, body unwinding, perception, and breathing strategies. Regardless of whether you understand it, your Chakras constantly grind away inside your body. They impact your psychological just as your physical state. By giving special consideration to these zones, you can move them to improve certain parts of your life.

Meditation is a skill that can be learned and honed, just like any other skill we try our hand at. It does not require any unique talents. On the other hand, it also needs to be approached without skepticism.

If you are new to meditation, you may initially feel awkward and uncomfortable. However, most people who experience the joys of meditation quickly learn to love it as a relaxing and enriching activity.

Meditation is an age-old practice established in ancient Indian traditions. It is practiced to open the mind to more profound intuition and perception. Several powerful meditations were developed explicitly to open the third eye and strengthen the pineal gland.

Meditation also helps you control your thoughts and mind, putting you, as the proponents of Buddhism believe, in control of your life. This is a highly empowering gift to have. So many things in life are out of our control—but by learning to control our thoughts, we can respond to situations wisely and calmly and make better choices. This skill becomes even more pronounced when your third eye chakra is awakened.

Meditation develops clarity, improves concentration, and is possibly one of the best ways to relieve stress. These are just a few of the benefits of meditation. All of the physical and mental benefits—as well as the research that confirms them—are just too numerous to list here.

How Does Meditation Work?

When you meditate, your brain enters an alpha wavelength state (which is different from the normal beta wavelength state with which the brain resonates). The mind becomes more open to receiving subtle messages and insights from our third eye in this calm and relaxed state. Regular meditation allows you to enter the alpha wavelength state more easily. Over time, you can receive more profound wisdom, knowledge, and information from the non-physical realm. It also helps strengthen spiritual gifts.

Types of Meditation

The types of meditation are varied and diverse. The most popular are Zen meditation, Vispana meditation, transcendental meditation, Taoist meditation, and mantra meditation. There is also a type of meditation for almost anything, from relieving pain and stress to meeting your higher guides. But ideally, meditation should be approached to achieve inner calm and deeper awareness—and the sheer bliss of just being able to forget the world and relax.

Meditations for the Third Eye

Meditation allows us to switch off the thinking and logical mind. When the reason is quietened and enters an alpha-level wavelength state, it becomes a filter for subtle insights and messages from the third eye.

All types of meditation are effective for opening the third eye. Guided meditation and any mindfulness meditation will work very well. However, the following are the most powerful for opening and nurturing the third eye.

Meditation 1: Trataka Meditation

This is an ancient meditation derived from the Tantra and Hatha yoga practices. In Sanskrit, Trataka means "to gaze" or "look."

● This meditation requires you to sit perfectly still on the floor with your legs crossed in the lotus position. If this is not comfortable, sit in a straight-backed chair where you can keep your spine straight.

● Close your eyes and breathe deeply from your belly for two-to-three minutes until your body is completely relaxed.

● Focus intensely on the area of your third eye chakra. Continue to focus on the site for a few moments.

● With both eyes still closed, draw them upwards towards the inner eye chakra as if you are looking at it. You may feel a strain in your eyes as you try and hold them in that position. You will know that it is the correct position when you think your eyes "lock" slightly above the bridge of your nose, and the work does not feel too strained.

● Keep your closed eyes in that position and slowly start counting backward from 100 (with about two seconds between each count).

● Keep your closed eyes focused on the third eye chakra until you have finished counting backward to zero.

● Draw your eyes back to their normal position and breathe deeply three times to ground yourself. Allow your eyes to return to their normal movement.

Chakra Healing

● Feel yourself become grounded and open your eyes. The meditation should last between ten-to-fifteen minutes.

Some people report seeing their thoughts as if they see a dream when doing this meditation. You may feel warmth in the area of the inner eye, which indicates that it is attracting energy. In addition, this is a compelling meditation for awakening the third eye, but it is also a great workout that keeps the eyes healthy.

Note: This meditation should be practiced in moderation to prevent the over-activation of the third eye chakra. Once a week will be enough to keep everything in balance.

Meditation 2: Body Scan Meditation for Third Eye Intuition

This meditation is oriented to increase your intuition through the third eye chakra.

● Sit in a comfortable position with your back straight.

● Close your eyes and do the mindful breathing exercise to ground yourself. This should take two to three minutes or until all the tension is released from your body and you feel completely relaxed.

● Start the body scan from the top of your head or the crown chakra. Focus on this area until you begin to notice the sensations there. This could be tingling, pressure, a slight warmth, burning, or buzzing. Don't worry if you don't feel anything the first couple of times you practice this meditation. Your mind will become trained to pick up on these sensations over time.

● When ready, move down to the forehead area from the front to the back of your head. Focus on this area—again, noticing any sensations there.

● When you are ready, move down to the eyes, the nose, the area above the mouth, and the mouth itself. Spend a few minutes on each side and notice the sensations.

● Continue the body scan by moving downwards and exploring every part of your body; chin, neck, shoulders, arms, torso, top of the stomach, lower belly, upper thighs, legs, and end with the feet.

● Do not react to or judge any negative sensations you may feel. Simply acknowledge them and move on.

● If you want, you can repeat the body scan, starting from the top of your head.

The meditation heightens intuition by making you more aware of the subtle sensations in your body. You may receive specific insights or "aha!" moments as you meditate—or even days after the meditation.

Meditation 3: Golden Ball of Light

● Sit in the lotus position or a comfortable chair with your back straight.

● Breathe deeply and feel the tension leave your muscles with every breath.

● Visualize a warm stream of energy flowing through your body from the top of your head to your toes. Continue to visualize and feel this energy slowly circulating your body.

● Next, direct your focus to the third eye chakra and the warm energy filling the space between your brows.

● Visualize the energy coming together to form a rotating ball of golden light in the center of your third eye chakra.

● Focus on the rotating ball and the beautiful golden light that emanates from it.

● When you feel ready, allow the light to expand until it fills all of your third eye chakras. Visualize it growing slowly until it emerges from your forehead in a bright ray of incandescent golden light.

● Gaze at the beautiful glow of light with your inner eye and notice any colors or pictures that appear within it.

● Simply acknowledge what you see without judgment.

● Now, still gazing into the light with your third eye, ask your third eye if it has a message for you. Take as much time as you need.

● When ready, bring yourself back to reality with deep breathing and slowly open your eyes.

Again, don't worry if you don't see anything the first few times you practice this meditation. The more you advance, the stronger the ray of light will become, and the images and messages from your third eye.

Meditation 4: Third Eye Awakening and Decalcifying the Pineal Gland

● Sit in a comfortable position and allow your body a few moments to settle and relax.

● Close your eyes, take a deep breath, and hold it for as long as possible, feeling your lungs' fullness. Exhale slowly through your mouth.

● Bring your entire focus to the third eye chakra. If it helps, you can visualize it as a small ball of light.

● Allow your senses to become vividly and intensely aware of everything around you; any sounds in the background, like voices or the hum of electrical appliances, the seat beneath you, the feel of your clothes against your skin, and any smells that may come to you.

● Allow your senses to experience these things while dismissing any thoughts about them entirely.

● Visualize your third eye absorbing and processing these sounds, smells, and sensations.

- When you are ready, end the meditation by taking a few deep breaths.

This meditation can be practiced daily. It energizes the third eye chakra and the pineal gland and heightens awareness and the senses.

Meditation 5: Mindfulness Breathing Cues

This is a great meditation to keep you grounded throughout your day and regularly mindful of your third eye.

- Choose a specific cue from your daily life, such as whenever you look in the mirror or brush your teeth when your phone rings or you have ended the call. It could be every time you look out the window or hear a dog bark or a car horn. Choose a cue that occurs regularly in your daily life—ideally, more than one.

- Each time they come up, breathe mindfully for a few minutes while focusing on your third eye chakra.

- Repeat the exercise whenever the cue occurs.

- This exercise allows you to relax and ground your overactive mind while checking in with your third eye.

Tips to Get the Most out of Meditation

Here are a few suggestions to help you meditate better. These are not mandatory rules but just valuable tips to consider.

Place. The ideal place to meditate should be relaxing and welcoming, with as little noise or disturbance as possible. It does not necessarily have to be indoors. Meditating in nature to the sounds of birds singing or waves sweeping onto the shore is a beautiful experience. The choice is up to you: just a calming environment that resonates with you.

Time. It is best to meditate each day simultaneously; having a consistent meditation schedule helps ground your mind and creates a regular pattern of time-out for the body and mind. Many people find that having a regular meditation schedule gives them something to look forward to during a hectic day. Their meditation time is a quiet, energizing haven from the havoc of daily life.

Position. Whether you choose to sit on the floor or in a chair, the important thing is that you are comfortable. The ideal situation is one where you can nod off if you want. Always give your body time to settle down and relax before you start, as fidgeting during meditation will break your focus.

● Try to clear your mind. Connecting with the third eye chakra and receiving information from the higher plane requires extreme clarity and calmness of the mind. This is easier said than done, especially if you are new to meditation. The best way to maintain transparency is to remain focused on the third eye for as long as possible during each meditation.

● Coming out of a meditative state is just as important as entering it. Never open your eyes and jump up. Always slowly bring your focus back to the physical world and ground yourself with a few deep breaths until you are fully aware of your surroundings.

● Take your time. Each meditation should last for at least 30 minutes.

● Wear loose, comfortable clothing and no shoes.

● Don't be alarmed when you suddenly receive a poignant message or thought from your third eye. This may disrupt your concentration.

● Learn how to sit in the proper lotus position, as it allows the best alignment of the body.

● Turn off cell phones, TVs, and other sources of distraction.

● Feel free to explore different forms of meditation, such as guided meditation and meditating to nature sounds or music or meditation that incorporates physical movement.

● Enjoy the experience.

A calm mind vibrates at a frequency that resonates with intuition. The more you meditate, the more your mind will learn to become quiet, allowing intuition to be heard more clearly. As your third eye begins to open and receive energy, so will your senses. You will start to develop crystal clear perception, as well as more and more moments of powerful intuition.

You will live more in the present moment, as these meditations are also great for boosting mindfulness. These gradual changes will be all the motivation you need to make meditation a part of your daily routine.

Chapter 4. The Pineal Gland

What Is the Pineal Gland and What Are Its Functions?

It is called pineal because it has the shape of a pineapple and is responsible for the production of serotonin. This substance regulates our circadian rhythm and controls the life cycles of the human body.

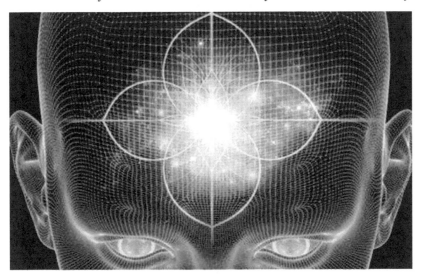

The pineal gland controls the action of light in our body and is located below the cerebral cortex, where two hemispheres of the brain meet. Knowing how to activate the pineal gland, people are more open to feelings of ecstasy and unity. They may also have a sense of understanding everything or a sudden understanding. In addition, when activated, people more quickly develop the ability to travel to other dimensions, known as astral projection or side observation.

According to Theosophy, the pineal gland is a source of clairvoyance and intuition and a portal for higher dimensions. The "third eye" gives us perception beyond the limits of general vision.

How to Activate the Pineal Gland

Activation can be achieved through yoga, meditation, and other esoteric methods. Here is an exercise that you can perform without leaving your home.

- Sit comfortably and place the index finger of your right hand between the eyebrows, marking the point.

- Concentrate on feeling a finger touch your forehead. Try to feel the heat and vibration at this point on your forehead.

- When you feel the pulsation at this point on your forehead, remove your finger and begin to deepen this feeling in your head.

- Then, visualize the bright light from the top of the head directly to the pulsating point in the center of the eyebrows and inside the skull.

- Concentrate on the sensation of pressure at the point on the forehead where light accumulates and enters. You may feel tinnitus and slight discomfort in the forehead, such as pressure.

This exercise activates the third eye and decalcifies the pineal gland. This exercise should be repeated daily or several times a day, as you wish. Little by little, you can develop your clarity in dreams, intuition, and clairvoyance.

Why Is the Pineal Gland Blocked?

Researchers claim that the main element responsible for the calcification of the pineal gland is fluoride in water. Also, chlorine, a low-nutrient diet, processed foods, electromagnetic fields (such as mobile phones), and environmental toxins are harmful to the pineal gland, ultimately calcined with calcium phosphate and calcium carbon magnesium, and ammonium phosphate.

Activities and exercises to decalcify the pineal gland

First, it is imperative to avoid calcium supplements for this to work. Artificial calcium supplements are the leading cause of calcification. Industrial food usually contains calcium in one form: calcium phosphate, calcium carbonate, or dicalcium phosphate. So do not eat "all done" anymore, and make smoothies! You will see why.

Raw cacao: Raw cacao contains many antioxidants, making it an excellent cleaner. It stimulates the pineal gland, the "third eye," and intuition.

Citric Acid: Squeezed lemon juice is excellent for detoxifying your pineal gland.

You can mix this lemon juice with spring water; it is refreshing and less bad for the teeth because of less acidity.

Garlic: A garlic cure is excellent for decalcification because garlic helps dissolve calcium and acts as an antibiotic. Garlic is also good for the immune system. During your cure treatment, increase your dose gradually to a head of garlic a day! Squeeze the garlic and mix it with apple cider vinegar or fresh lemon juice to avoid bad breath.

Boron: Boron is excellent for detoxifying and cleansing the pineal gland. It is also effective in removing fluoride. You can try adding 1/4 teaspoon of sodium borate (borax) to your green tea. A cheap source of boron is classic borax, which can be purchased in most supermarkets. Borax should be taken in tiny quantities, in pure water, with no more than 1/32 to 1/4 teaspoon of borax per liter of water. The safe and effective way is to consume this mixture in small quantities throughout the day.

Chlorella: Did you know that chlorella has a phytochemical element that can effectively rebuild nerve damage in the brain and nervous system; in this way, chlorella is used to recover patients with Alzheimer's and Parkinson's disease. You can live just by eating microalgae like Chlorella and Spirulina; they are superfoods from 2 to 8 microns, so the size of the blood cells.

The fact that chlorella is green comes from its chlorophyll content. It does not contain refined carbohydrates, includes a high level of digestive protein, contains fatty acids, is not bad fat, and contains chlorophyll. It is said that chlorella is a perfect whole. In addition to being a complete protein, it has all the vitamins; B, vitamin C, vitamin E, and the main minerals (such as iron and zinc in amounts large enough to be considered complimentary); it has been found that it improves the immune system, improves digestion and detoxification; accelerate healing, protect against radiation, it helps in the prevention of degenerative diseases, helps in the treatment of illness, and relieves arthritis pain, because of its nutritional value, and helps the success of many diets to lose weight.

Zeolite: Zeolite is a mineral found in the ancient seabed and derived from volcanic rocks. Its honeycomb-shaped molecules can safely capture large quantities of toxins and expel them through the urinary tract. It can be considered +++ clay. It is delivered in excellent powder obtained by a special micronization process.

For excess calcium, we will also focus on vitamin K2, which acts as a regulator of calcium in the tissues, promoting the fixation of calcium in the matrix of the bones and cleaning all the deposits useless.

Avoid all foods that contain pesticides: To detoxify the pineal gland, the best is to make a cure composed mainly of raw fruits and vegetables, but of course, without pesticides. The meat also contains pesticides, often when the animals eat cereals or grass. Some people recommend vegetarian diets to detoxify the body or protect the pineal gland against potentially harmful substances. Yet some meats are still recommended, so how to manage priorities?

If you cannot pronounce the chemical name, it is probably bad for your health. Among these chemicals, we find:

Artificial sweeteners such as aspartame (there are slightly more natural sweeteners like xylitol).

Refined white sugar (replaced by brown sugar, honey, molasses, agave syrup, maple syrup, or cooked wine).

Deodorants and products against foul odors, industrially produced

Dental mouthwashes (replace with saltwater, enough!)

Chemical cleaning products

Activate Melatonin Production

Although there is no objective conclusive evidence, many people believe that melatonin helps eliminate fluoride by increasing the decalcification of the pineal gland, which helps to degrade existing calcification.

Our body uses an essential amino acid, tryptophan, extracted from the food proteins we absorb to produce melatonin. Tryptophan is then converted to serotonin, which will itself be transformed by the pineal gland into melatonin, which the liver will then metabolize. Melatonin limits oxidation in all cellular compartments and increases other antioxidant enzymes' activity, so it has an anti-aging effect.

Tips to Naturally Maintain a Good Level of Melatonin

Melatonin is synthesized chiefly at night, and the absence of light stimulates its production.

At night, expose yourself as little as possible to an excess of light, which could lower or even suppress melatonin concentration. Avoid any light source (avoid sleeping with a night light, for example). The light disrupts the production of melatonin. If you need a light in the hallway or the bathroom, use a light that filters the blue spectrum. (Yellow light bulbs).

During the day, melatonin production at night will be favored if you expose yourself to the sunlight.

Eat foods that promote melatonin production: melatonin is synthesized from serotonin, derived from tryptophan, an essential amino acid. It is, therefore, necessary to focus on foods containing tryptophan. What are they?

Parsley, pumpkin seeds, cheese, cod, parmesan, milk and soy, turkey, pineapple, eggs, dates, lettuce, bananas, plums, rice, corn, oatmeal, walnuts and hazelnuts, tomatoes, potatoes, and red wine are rich in tryptophans. Therefore, it is necessary to consume these foods regularly; therefore, it is essential to obtain an optimal serotonin level regularly. For example, nut consumption increases blood melatonin levels in rats by a factor of three.

The Miracles of the Nettle

100 grams of fresh nettle leaves have all the recommended daily contributions of calcium and iron, as well as six times the RDA of pro-vitamin A and four times that of vitamin C. Reason for which the nettle is to be consumed instead in the morning or at midday than in the evening.

Some are rare components, such as choline acetyltransferase, an enzyme that synthesizes acetylcholine, and nettle is the only known plant to possess this enzyme. If one is not yet convinced of it, it is proof that the nettle is not a plant.

Other Basic Methods With Which You Can Start Work on the Activation of the Pineal Gland

1. Take the maximum from night and day

For the development of the pineal gland, a person's sleep schedule and wakefulness mustn't go astray. The most helpful sleep regimen for the pineal gland is falling asleep early (around 10 pm) and early rise (ideally, at dawn).

In addition to sleeping in the dark, it is also necessary to learn how to maximize the benefits in the daytime - more o, often to be in the sun (or at least sit by the window).

2. Electromagnetic fields are your enemies

Electromagnetic fields haunt us everywhere: we even carry them in our pockets (telephones) and spend leisure time and working hours with them (computers). Of course, such an impact negatively affects the development of the pineal gland, so it is essential to use every opportunity to stay away not only from the bustle of the city but also from worldly goods.

3. Meditate whenever possible

Meditation is a powerful practice that can change a person's life. It is scientifically proven that it benefits the state of mind and the entire human body, helping to find harmony, know oneself, and be distracted from the bustle. During meditation, focus on the pineal gland, the Third Eye.

Meditate regularly and chant mantras. Singing causes resonance in the nose, making the pineal gland work. The more exciting it is, the more youth hormones are secreted into your body. The sound "OM" resonates with the fourth chakra, known as the center of the heart of the place of Unconditional Love. The repetition of OM opens the path to universal and cosmic consciousness. You can repeat it for 5 minutes, 10 minutes, or any other time.

4. Do yoga

Yoga pays considerable attention to the development of the pineal gland since the pineal gland is considered the same antenna with which our brain can perceive the most crucial information from the outside. The most helpful posture for pineal gland development is Shashankasana, i.e., hare pose, as it stimulates the pineal gland and upper chakra. Thanks to this asana, one can also improve memory and concentration.

5. Use such aids as crystals

Amethyst, laser quartz, moonstone, purple sapphire, tourmaline, rhodonite, and sodalite. In general, any natural stone of blue, indigo, or purple colors can be used to activate the pineal gland and work on Ajna and Sahasrara.

Take the stone and place it between the eyebrows for 15 minutes. Try to look at it with your eyes closed. Maintain a maximum concentration of these 15 minutes. It is perfect if you can do this under direct access to the sun - then its rays will pass through the stone into the pineal gland. Moreover, it will be easier to concentrate on the light.

6. Use aromatic oils to stimulate the pineal gland and alleviate the general mental state

They also help with meditations and various other practices. Using lavender, sandalwood, frankincense, pine, lotus, and wormwood is recommended. Oils can be inhaled, ignited in unique lamps, sprayed, or added to the bathwater.

7. Use magnets for detoxification

Just put it between your eyebrows for several hours. They attract alkali and thus remove calcium crystals from the pineal gland.

8. Forget about alcohol, nicotine, and caffeine

These stimulants interfere with the established melatonin production system. The less you consume them, the better for you and your sleep.

Some drugs can disrupt the production of melatonin can also disrupt melatonin production - do not forget to consult a doctor.

9. Clear your mind about the new moon.

The new moon is an excellent time for all kinds of undertakings and pineal gland development. If you clear your mind, you will feel how the pineal gland activates and brings calm, and balance to your body and cleans it. That is why yoga's day of the new moon is of such great importance: yogis are fully committed to spiritual practices, not being distracted even by eating food and water.

10. Make it a habit to look at the sun for 15 minutes immediately after it rises and at sunset daily.

Chapter 5. Ways to Heal and Balance The Chakras

You have now understood the techniques to heal and balance your chakras. This chapter will deal with the healing and balancing of individual chakras. If you know that any specific chakra in your body is not functioning correctly, you can take steps to clear the chakra's blockage and balance the energy flow.

This chapter will tell you the specific tools to heal the chakras and suggest vital lifestyle and behavioral changes. By incorporating these changes, you can expect faster healing and a more excellent balance in life and your energies. You can expect more rapid recovery and a more excellent balance in life and your points by incorporating these changes; you can expect more rapid recovery and a more excellent balance in life and your issues. You'll find that controlling your mind and emotions will become more accessible, and it'd be easy to remain stress-free and happy.

Root Chakra Healing

Lifestyle Changes

- Practice Earth Sitting and Hiking

To balance the root chakra, you must establish a close connection with the earth, as the physical element of this chakra is the earth. You may feel ungrounded when this chakra gets blocked or out of balance. Try to be as close to the planet for some time every day. Earth Sitting is an excellent way to establish a connection with the earth. You can also go on hiking trips to connect you with the planet.

- Do Gardening

Gardening is another way to establish a deep connection with the earth. While gardening, every plant you handle has its roots deep inside the planet. You get to develop direct contact with the seeds. You also need to take much earth in the process of gardening, and that also helps in restoring balance.

- Increase Physical Activity

An imbalance in this chakra can make you inactive. Excessive and sudden weight gain is one of the side effects of inequality in the root chakra. To restore balance, it is essential essential essential that you incorporate much physical activity in your life. If your work involves intense physical labor, it's ok; otherwise, join a gym. Sweating every day is very important to bring balance. If you are trying to restore the balance in your root chakra while leading a sedentary lifestyle, you are up for a great challenge.

- Try Walking Barefoot on Grass

Walking barefoot in the grass in gardens is another way to establish a sensory connection with this earth. It is a very soothing and relaxing exercise. There are several other health benefits of this activity too.

However, it is perfect for healing the root chakra. After the walks, you'll feel more grounded, rational, and secure.

• Eat Red Fruits

RED IS THE COLOR OF THIS CHAKRA. EATING RED FRUITS AND KEEPING RED THINGS AROUND YOU WILL HELP YOU HEAL THIS CHAKRA FASTER.

Yoga Asanas

Several important yoga asanas can help faster healing and balance this chakra. Some of them are:

• Standing Forward Bend

• Head-to-Knee pose

• Supported Corpse Pose

• Warrior I

• Warrior II

• Tree pose

• Chair pose

• Supported Child's pose

Meditation

Meditation is an excellent way to heal and balance the chakras. You should focus on the pelvic region while meditating and connect it with your third eye chakra. Try to expand and contract this region consciously, which would also help stimulate the energies in this chakra.

Crystals

Black tourmaline, bloodstone, hematite, obsidian, ruby, garnet, onyx, lodestone, fire agate, red jasper, and smoky quartz can help restore the balance in this chakra.

Essential Oils

Myrrh, patchouli, sandalwood, and spikenard are essential oils that effectively heal the root chakra.

Sacral Chakra Healing

Lifestyle Changes

•   Give Proper Vent to Your Sexual Energy

This chakra is highly bent toward enjoying the bounties of this world. The physical location of this chakra is very close to your genitals, and hence, the sexual energy in your body can become unbalanced quickly. You must give proper vent to your sexual stamina. You may develop negativity if your sexual energy is not getting the appropriate expression. Your temperament may change, and your social behavior can become aggressive. You must have a balanced and active sexual life to keep this chakra in sync.

•   Explore New Things

This chakra likes to explore new things. However, if the energies in this chakra are out of balance, you may lack interest in everything. The easy way to restore balance is to force yourself to do new things. Try new fresh food, clothes, and places. Change and variety will help in healing the chakras faster.

•   Try Creative Pursuits

This chakra has a high potential to be creative. This is the chakra of the explorers. It has great creative energy trapped inside. If you try new and innovative things, it can help stimulate the energy centers of this chakra.

- Get Involved in Community Service

This chakra likes to live for itself, but this can also make a person self-serving, unrestrained, and indifferent. All these things can lead to imbalance. It would help if you got involved with community service to keep your sacral chakra balanced.

- Take Help from Reiki Healing

Reiki healing is a terrific way to find the blockages in this chakra and resolve them. If you have developed a distaste for everything all of a sudden, you must consult a reiki healer immediately for help.

- Orange Color

THE COLOR OF THIS CHAKRA IS ORANGE. IT IS ONE OF THE MOST VIBRANT AND FLAMBOYANT COLORS. IT GIVES YOU A DISTINCT FLAVOR AND PERSONALITY. IF THIS CHAKRA IS OUT OF BALANCE, EATING ORANGE COLOR FRUITS AND KEEPING THE THINGS OF THIS COLOR NEAR YOU CAN HELP IN RESTORING THE ENERGY BALANCE.

Yoga Asanas

Some of the essential yoga asanas for healing chakra imbalance are:

- Happy baby pose
- Child's pose
- Downward-facing dog
- Cow face pose
- Bound angle pose
- Open-angle pose
- Warrior poses
- Four limb staff pose

Meditation

You must focus on the area just below your navel when you meditate. Try to feel the orange light there. Inculcate positive thoughts and let go of the repressed memories and emotions.

Crystals

Orange tourmaline, sunstone, carnelian, moonstone, and amber are some crystals that can help heal this chakra.

Essential Oils

Patchouli, rosewood, sandalwood, and ylang-ylang are essential oils that can treat the imbalance in this chakra.

Solar Plexus Chakra Healing

Lifestyle Changes

•   Practice healthy boundaries

An imbalance in this chakra may make you forget personal and professional boundaries. The best way to balance this chakra is to start practicing healthy boundaries in your personal and professional lives. Don't try to encroach on the space of others. The more you follow the boundaries edges, the easier it will get to lead a healthy life. Your solar plexus chakra will start settling down if you bring down the aggressive and encroaching tendencies.

•   Sungazing

This chakra gets its power from the sun and illuminates inside you like a sun. If you are feeling low in energy in this chakra or unable to focus on your projects, try sun gazing early in the morning at the time of dawn when the sun is crimson red. It will give power to your chakra.

•   Sunbathing

In the same way as sun gazing, sunbathing is equally beneficial for treating the imbalance in the solar plexus chakra. It will also help you in getting rid of several skin issues.

- Physically active routine

It is essential to keep this chakra energized; you maintain a physically active routine. This chakra doesn't work well in people who live very sedentary lifestyles. This is the chakra of the hardworking lot. Try to get involved in some job that requires intense physical work or devote some time to the gym or play outdoor sports.

- Breaking the comfort zone

This is a chakra that sets new norms. It makes you try harder and excel in everything you do. This chakra will get out of balance if you adopt a lifestyle that doesn't want to leave your comfort zone and take on new challenges. To keep this chakra active, keep taking on new challenges. Come out of your comfort zone and do things you haven't tried before.

- Yellow

YELLOW IS THE COLOR OF THIS CHAKRA, AND HENCE, YELLOW-COLORED FRUITS AND THINGS IN THIS COLOR WILL BE BENEFICIAL FOR RESTORING THE ENERGY BALANCE IN THIS CHAKRA.

Yoga Asanas

Some of the important essential yoga asanas for healing chakra imbalance are:

- Pranayam or breathing techniques

- Bellows breath

- Boat pose

- Half-boat pose

- Sun salutation

- Cat pose

- Cow pose

Meditation

You can practice body scan meditation and breathing meditation to heal this chakra. These meditation techniques help you feel the raw power in your body, and you can get hold of your physicality much better.

Crystals

Yellow Citrine, yellow topaz, yellow tiger's eye, amber, rutilated quartz, and yellow agate can be beneficial crystals for healing the energy imbalance in this chakra.

Essential Oils

Rosewood, lemon, lavender, roman chamomile, and rosemary are essential oils for healing this chakra imbalance.

Heart Chakra Healing

Lifestyle Changes

- Learn new art forms

The heart chakra is the center of creation. If this chakra is out of balance, the best way to restore energy balance is to ignite your creative spark. Try to learn some new creative art forms. Listening to music, learning to play musical instruments, drawing, painting, singing, dancing, and all other creative ways to express your energies can help you stimulate the energy center in this chakra.

- Treat yourself well

This chakra can be out of balance if you are not getting due attention or care. Emotional stability is essential for this chakra as it is susceptible in nature. To restore balance, you must indulge yourself in self-care. Treat yourself frequently. Give yourself enough of 'me time.' Don't ignore your needs for long. Repressed emotions can have a very negative impact on this chakra's energy balance.

- Love someone

This chakra has a deep longing for love. People start feeling unloved, undesired, and unwanted whenever there is an imbalance in this chakra. To keep this chakra in balance, love someone. It isn't essential to love a person in particular. Invest your love into anything. Love pets, art forms, passions, or people around you.

- Remain motivated

It would help if you kept yourself motivated to keep this chakra balanced. Negativity, depression, and regret are some of the emotions that can trip the balance of this chakra. Listen to motivational talks and indulge yourself in activities that invoke optimism. Your positive attitude can help a lot in keeping this chakra balanced.

- Do charity or social work

Charity or social work are also great ways to keep this chakra working smoothly. The more you work for others, the more receptive you are to positive energies. You become accepting in nature. This is a great way to keep the heart chakra in balance.

- Go in the wild

Spending time in the wild is a great way to give your heart chakra a boost. Nature has a significant healing impact on the heart chakra. It restores the positive balance in the body. You should take frequent breaks from your routine life and return to the lap of nature.

- Accept new people

This chakra works best when you are accepting of nature. Do not have rigid ideas in your mind about people. Be more accepting and embracing. Accept people for whom they are without attaching qualifications. This can help you in keeping the balance in the chakra intact.

•   Green

THE COLOR OF THIS CHAKRA IS GREEN. EATING GREEN FRUITS AND VEGETABLES AND KEEPING GREEN COLOR AROUND YOU WILL HELP IN HEALING THIS CHAKRA FASTER.

Yoga Asanas

Some of the essential yoga asanas for healing chakra imbalance are:

•   Eagle pose

•   Arm balances

•   Camel pose

•   Seated spinal twist

Meditation

A guided meditation that helps you embrace nature is the best for restoring balance in this chakra. Loving and kind meditation is one of the best ways to heal this chakra. When working on this chakra, you must keep your mind filled with sweet emotions. It would help if you didn't form too many ideas in your mind, as this chakra can make you imagine weird things.

Crystals

Rose quartz, jade, green calcite, emerald, green kyanite, and green tourmaline are some crystals that can help heal and balance this chakra.

Essential Oils

Ylang-ylang, rose, palmarosa, bergamot, geranium, neroli, lavender, and melissa are essential oils that can heal the imbalance in this chakra.

Throat Chakra Healing

Lifestyle Changes

• Don't lie

This first chakra takes you on an intellectual and spiritual awakening. It is also a chakra with much power vested in the throat. If you lie a lot, the throat chakra will get affected. This chakra doesn't support lying. You will not only start losing the power in your voice, but you may also start having mental clarity issues. The most important way to restore the energy balance in this chakra is to stop lying in your day-to-day life.

• Develop the habit of discussion

The more you discuss things with others, the greater the influence of this chakra will be. Discussions with people help this chakra in becoming more expressive. Do not keep your thoughts to yourself. Indulge yourself in healthy conversations with wise people. You will find that your mental clarity will increase, and the impact of throat chakra will also become visible.

• Work on the art of public speaking

Public speaking is the forte of the throat chakra. A person with energies centered in the throat chakra will be a great orator. However, if your throat chakra is not working correctly, working on the art of public speaking will help you in balancing your throat chakra.

• Become more expressive

Start expressing your feelings. The more you keep your feelings to yourself, the greater the burden you'll put on your throat chakra. Don't keep suppressing your emotions. Speak your heart out, and that would help in restoring which would help restore the balance in the throat chakra.

- Sky gazing

Gazing at the blue sky can also be very helpful in restoring the balance in the throat chakra. The light blue sky energizes your throat chakra and helps in faster healing.

- Blue

BLUE THINGS HELP HEAL THIS CHAKRA, AND YOU CAN EAT BLUE FRUITS, AS WELL AS KEEP BLUE THINGS AROUND YOU FOR FASTER HEALING OF THE CHAKRA.

Yoga Asanas

Some of the essential yoga asanas for healing chakra imbalance are:

- Bridge pose
- Triangle pose
- Camel Pose
- Warrior pose
- Extended side angle
- Plow pose
- Shoulder stand

Meditation

Meditation while chanting the seed mantra of this chakra, 'Ham,' is beneficial. Even guided meditations with visualizations are very helpful in healing the imbalance in this chakra.

The longer you meditate on this chakra, the better the results. Your prime focus should be on bringing clarity to your speech.

Crystals

Lapis lazuli, iolite, turquoise, blue kyanite, aquamarine, celestite, and sodalite are important crystals for treating imbalance in this chakra.

Essential Oils

Rosemary, frankincense, lavender, hyssop, and German chamomile are essential oils used to heal this chakra.

Third Eye Chakra Healing

Lifestyle Changes

• Don't limit yourself

The third eye chakra brings you immense possibilities. It opens millions of doors in front of you to do the same thing. It helps you in looking at things differently. If you start limiting yourself and questioning every action, you might put undue pressure on this chakra. Start thinking more courageously. Don't think with a limited perspective. Think in broader and broader terms. Don't think just about yourself; think about the greater good too. Expanding your limits of thinking can help address the issues in this chakra.

• Work on balancing your brain

The third eye chakra is closely related to your brain and mental faculties. However, when the third eye chakra is active, it needs much activity to channel the energy. You must engage yourself in brain-balancing activities to sharpen your brain.

• Work on your root chakra

Keeping your root chakra strong is crucial for bringing balance to your third eye chakra. This chakra can thin the line between reality and imagination. You can start imagining impossible things. You may not remain grounded and may begin making impossible plans. You may also face problems dealing with the energies around you if your root chakra is not strong. To keep your third eye chakra balanced, you should also control your root chakra to be stable and functioning.

• Don't rely on daydreaming

The third eye chakra can make you delusional at times. People start living in an imaginary world, and all that happens when they are not ready to handle energies of this magnitude. Your mind and body should be prepared to deal with the points of this intensity. You should stop daydreaming and start living in the real world.

• Be careful of negative influences

The third eye chakra increases your field of perception. This means that you start feeling the presence of other forms of energy around you. You begin interacting with them more frequently. If your energy field is not very strong or your root chakra is weak, you may be influenced by those energies. It is essential that when your third eye chakra is out of balance, you remain careful of the kind of people and energies you interact with. It would help if you immediately started work on strengthening your energy field.

• Indigo

INDIGO IS THE COLOR OF THIS CHAKRA, AND IT WOULD BE HELPFUL IF YOU COULD KEEP THINGS OF THIS COLOR AROUND YOU. IT WILL HELP STRENGTHEN YOUR ENERGY FIELD.

Yoga Asanas

There is no specific yoga that is more helpful in enhancing this chakra. It would help if you focused on raising your consciousness level as much as possible. This chakra is more associated with intellectual and spiritual realization and less with physical manifestations. Try to build a greater focus.

Meditation

You can do specific third-eye chakra meditations to better balance this chakra. It would help if you reduced the influence of negative energies around you when you sit for meditation, as your energy field can sometimes get weak. You must not fear anything while meditating, even if negative thoughts come to mind.

Crystals

Lepidolite, sugilite, lapis lazuli, amethyst, fluorite, tanzanite, clear quartz, star sapphire, and kyanite can help balance and heal this chakra.

Essential Oils

Frankincense, lavender, and sandalwood are effective in balancing this chakra.

Crown Chakra Healing

Lifestyle Changes

- Give respect to your elders

This is the topmost chakra that is associated with spiritual consciousness. If this chakra keeps functioning balanced, you will be highly respected, have a healing touch, and possess great wisdom. You would always remain in a state of utmost pleasantness. It is like being blissful around the clock, irrespective of the situation around you. However, if this chakra malfunctions, it can frustrate you. The best way to balance this chakra is to respect others, especially your elders. When you show respect to your elders, it fills you with humility. That negates the buildup of negative energy.

- Be thankful

Remain thankful for everything in life. Don't be grumpy or sad. The more pleasant you maintain the more balanced the energies in this chakra will be.

- Do more charity

The more you give to others, the more you receive love and respect. Whatever you give away is the real wealth you can earn in terms of spiritual consciousness. Therefore, it is vital to remain involved in charitable activities.

There are few physical ways and tools to balance or heal this chakra. This chakra is almost outside your body and isn't controlled by material things. The best way to keep this chakra balanced is to practice yoga and meditation. Both these activities can help keep this chakra healthy and balanced.

Chapter 6. Guided Meditation Techniques to Open the Third Eye

The previous section states that the third eye is above the eyebrows. It is one of the responsible ones responsible for visual abilities, which include seeing visions, flashes, and symbols. To increase the power of the clairvoyance abilities, you need to apply meditation as one of the vital techniques. Besides meditation, you need to focus on your third eye to trust the exterior experiences to ensure that the third eye is open if it is closed.

Sometimes, it may not open immediately, and you must ask it to spread until it does. When it opens, you will feel calm, and warmth runs through your body. The feeling will result from the body part opening that was blocked. It has to be awake so that things will run smoothly.

You need to be preoccupied with a perfect approach to open the third eye for your close to open. It is essential since it functions as an ethereal bridge to connect the physical and the spiritual worlds. The soul makes you a unique and active person, and you must ensure access through the opening of the third eye. It will unlock higher knowledge, and you will appreciate your experiences from time to time. The third eye does not function independently but with the hypothalamus gland. That means that it will influence some of your vital biological functions.

Chakra Healing

Opening your third eye opens the doorway to the wisdom stored in your soul. When you meditate to open your third eye, you will undoubtedly have the best spiritual guide. Powerful awakening will happen, and you will appreciate the gift in you that is about to take you to higher levels spiritually. You can choose to go the meditation way to open your third eye. It can be done either independently or with an expert to guide you. When doing the guided meditation, the expert will advise you on some steps to ensure your eye will open. Some of the techniques include and are not limited to the following;

Step 1: Choose a Location

For meditation to hit the primary target, you must look for a place with minimal disturbances. A quiet place is all you need to start with. When choosing the site, you must ensure that you will be consistent. The person to guide you on the meditation should be compatible with you. Your body and mind need to get used to the place you choose. You should select a position in charge of activating your third eye. That, too, you should consider when choosing the location.

Step 2: Choose the Time with an Intention

After the first step, work on the second step, selecting the time you will be going for the guided meditation sessions. You will need to go for the sessions daily to be helpful. The time you decide to have the sessions should be reasonable. It would help if you remained fixed at the time that you chose. Think of the time that will suit you best, and your body and mind should be free and in a relaxed mood. You need to avoid scheduling the sessions immediately before or after your meals. When you choose a morning, it will work best for you. But that does not mean that any other time is not appropriate. All that is needed when you choose any additional time besides morning is you maintain consistency.

Step 3: Make Some Stretches Before You Begin the Meditation Session

It would help if you did some stretches before the meeting since you will have to sit longer in the room. You can have a more relaxing time as you meditate on how to open your third eye to realize the power in you. Doing this before getting into the meditation sessions will go to a deeper length of your mental framework. You can try bending over as you try to touch the toes for at least a minute. You can stretch your arms above the head as a way of relaxing. Do not forget to lay on your back and ensure that your feet are in the air at ninety degrees with the body.

Step 4: Position Yourself

Meditation cannot take place while you are standing. It would help if you adopted a sitting position where you feel relaxed and cross your legs. If you find this posture disturbing and uncomfortable, decide to change and take one that is not difficult for you. A position that will make you relax and focus quickly on your breathing, as well as meditation, is what you need to consider. It would help if you sat on the floor while you closed your legs to meditate better on how to open your third eye and access the hidden spiritual treasures. Your chest should be open and your back straight. Consider placing your hands either on the knees or the la,p depending on the position you will better. Your head needs to be upright and closed, and your eyes gently, so you can get into the world of meditation.

Step 5: Relax

After you adopt a posture that you feel comfortable in, the next logical thing you need to do is give your body a chance to settle. Meditation cannot take place when you are not relaxed. Be mindful of how your body is feeling, and if there are feelings that you need to work on before the actual meditation, do that. Make sure your entire body is relaxed and ready to begin the session. Pay attention to all body parts, each at a time, as you sit and relax. Shift your mind from any worry you may have and be ready to pay attention to the present moment. As you breathe in and out, make sure you feel your body expanding and contracting when you take every breath.

Step 6: Breath

Breathing is a crucial technique in meditation. Be focused on how you breathe in and out and put your full attention on living. Take deep breaths from time to time on the count of three as you inhale and exhale.

Step 7: Empty the Mind

At this point, you will begin focusing on the third eye, which is at the center of the forehead. With still, your eyes are closed; move your eyes toward the third eye. It would help if you focused without moving your eyes from that position throughout the meditation process. Remaining on the emphasis, count from one hundred, moving backward but do not worry if you cannot experience the third eye at that moment. It can take quite some time to get used to the meditation process. It can take longer to activate your third eye, but that should not worry you. All you need to do is maintain consistency; everything will work out with time.

Step 8: Access the Third Eye

When you are through with counting from a hundred backward, it is time that you try to access the sight. Make sure that you have maintained the focus in the previous steps so that this point will be a success. When you have the attention, you will notice that everything is dark apart from your third eye. When the vision is active, your brain will be relaxed and function on an entirely new level. All the sides of the brain will work in unison, and you will feel the energy surrounding you. You will feel a new energy level running through your body and around you. That is when you will know that you got access to your third eye. When you focus on an object or image strongly, that is time that you know that you are accessing the eye. Your mind needs to be fully consumed by the entity or idea for that to happen.

Step 9: Work on Experiencing Your Third Eye

Everyone has a different way of reacting to the activation of their third eye. You may experience your mind flashing visual effects and any other experiences and scenes you may have come through. If they can be laid out, it can be a way of seeing your thoughts, like how they appear. As you continue focusing on experiencing your third eye, you will slowly work on opening the eye.

Step 10: Maintain Your Focus on the Third Eye

It would help if you remained focused on the third eye for about ten to fifteen minutes. You may have a headache during the very first sessions but know that it is a normal thing that will happen to almost every beginner. There is no need to worry since the headache will be no more as you get used to the practice. You must train yourself to fully appreciate your third eye and maintain focus on one image. Amongst the pictures that will appear in your mind, pay attention to the one you choose. Make sure you work to keep the mind centered on the focus that you have made. You will find it open slowly when you focus on the third eye. That means you achieved your aim when you decided to meditate. Your third eye will open, and you will have a great experience with the precious gift in you.

Step 11: Get out of Meditation Slowly

When you finally achieve what you intended, the next thing is to bring yourself out of the meditation. Remove your focus from your third eye slowly and still maintain the relaxed mood you were in when during the whole process. Your guide will tell you that you must be aware of your breath. You can choose to count to focus on your breathing when bringing your mind from the meditation. Open your eyes slowly to end the entire process finally.

In cases when you need to open your third eye any other time, practice the above steps, and it will be easier this time. That is because it will not be the first time to do that. Work on making your body feel better and become in touch with the inner self. However, that will not immediately come since you need to practice the meditation process, going to greater heights. You will be more in touch with yourself and the energy in and around you. That is the main idea of meditating to open your third eye.

You will experience signs to show that your eye is open. Once you manage to open the third eye, you will no longer have self-doubt. You will have the desire to research as well as learn more. You will be more sensitive to spirits and may see them occasionally. You will be wiser and will learn from your past mistakes. The chances are that you will be more creative and feel divine inspiration will achieve great potential. You will enjoy and experience a healthy life once you connect with the spirits. You will find the world a place of harmony to live in and appreciate your life more. When you finish the self-journey, do not be mean but work to show other buddies with a similar gift to you the way of self-realization.

Chapter 7.Secret Tips for Third Eye Chakra

We've discussed the Third Eye in the context of the whole chakra system. But this chakra is quite different from the others around it. The five chakras below concern how you interact with and experience the material world. But the Third Eye is something else: the gateway to a whole new, spiritual world.

The Third Eye is perhaps the chakra most shrouded in mystery. Much of our knowledge about it has been passed down throughout history, with some of the knowledge dating back to ancient civilizations.

The Ancient Greek doctor and philosopher Galen wrote about the third eye back in ancient times. He reports that his colleagues say the pineal gland, located next to the third eye, regulates psychic energy. He only saw the gland as controlling blood flow, however.

In Hindu culture, the god Shiva and other deities are represented as having a literal third eye on their forehead. This symbolizes enlightenment, the ability of these gods to see into the higher realms.

The Third Eye also crops up in Ancient Egyptian culture as the sacred Eye of Ra and Horus. This eye was drawn on the center of the forehead on sarcophagi, the coffins in which the mummies of the pharaohs were placed. This, similarly, was seen as the eye of the critical gods Ra and Horus, symbolizing a connection to the divine.

The Third Eye is often symbolized as a pinecone because of its eye-like shape and connection to sacred geometry. In this case, we see a lot of pinecone imagery in ancient civilizations. Ancient Sumerian gods are often depicted with a pinecone, as is the ancient Greek god Dionysus is associated with expanded consciousness and moving beyond the material world.

Additionally, there is a recurring symbol of two serpents rising to meet a pinecone in the ancient world. In Ancient Egypt, this was the staff of Osiris. This can be interpreted as the energy in the body rising to meet the Third Eye and enlightenment.

In the Catholic Church, the pinecone carries excellent symbolic weight even today. You can see one atop the staff of the Pope.

The presence of pinecones and serpents in such abundance has caused some to suspect that the pinecone was the fruit that Eve ate in the tale of Genesis that led to Adam and Eve being expelled from the Garden of Eden, the Fall of Man in Biblical legend. If that is true, then the presence of the Third Eye has had an undeniable impact on civilizations across the globe.

You may be a bit confused about what precisely the Third Eye is. Not to worry -- it's pretty hard to conceptualize these aspects of the spiritual world. Simply put, it allows you to see into worlds and states of consciousness that would otherwise be shut off to you. Seeing these things and understanding them is an integral step on the path to enlightenment.

It is referred to by other names, including the inner eye and the eye of knowledge. To utilize your third eye is to have access to not only the inner worlds of yourself but the higher planes of existence in our universe.

The aim of opening the third eye is the same as most good spiritual healing -- to gain deeper insight into yourself and the world, to 'be more. You have probably heard that humans currently only use a fraction of their potential contained in their minds. You may have heard of Plato's myth of the cave, in which humans who had lived their whole life in a cave thought that the shadows on the wall were the real world. This remains relevant today. Most people can't begin to think of the wonder that they could see if they allowed themselves to expand their horizons and walk amid the real world, the spiritual world. Instead, they remained trapped in the material world.

In India, the coconut was a potent symbol in several rituals. It has 'three eyes.' If you look at a coconut, you can see the indentations this refers to. According to the symbolism, two are 'blind,' meaning they don't produce mile when pierced, while the third one is the one you stick to gain the coconut's milk. Similarly, the third eye is the door you punch, showing you to the higher planes. This eye gives you the sight to know yourself and the world around you to the degree that goes most conventional methods of scientific psychological analysis or any way based on interpreting life with your mind grounded in the material world.

Before we get into the procedures to open the third eye, you must have a framework of how you will experience these revelations. It's important to remember to trust your experience. Since there is nothing to believe on the other side of the doors of perception, there is nothing to doubt, either! You don't want to take up all your time worrying about whether you may be seeing what you see by any objective standards. Trust your experience.

Similarly, when you experience it, you don't want to analyze it. Not yet, anyway. You only want to take in the revelations that you are being given. After the experience, you will have plenty of time to break down what happened. Additionally, the rational analysis only goes so far from the third eye. You will receive the most dividends by silently pondering and digesting your experiences. By planting the seeds, your knowledge will develop into a greater understanding of the spiritual world.

So -- I can imagine the question you have. How do I open it? Well, unfortunately, it's not easy. However, it's possible for anyone who knows these techniques to do it. It just takes practice and a willingness to learn from the wisdom of the past.

The truth is that although having the correct methods for expanding your consciousness is essential, it's not style or technique that matters as far as opening the third eye is concerned. The most significant difference is whether or not you have the capacity to persist along a path. Those who have reached states of great enlightenment have done so because they continued to the point where no earthly obstacle could stand in their way, and the doors to knowledge became clear to them. This kind of dogged persistence is one of the best qualities you can develop. Even starting from a beginner's level, it is by constant attention to expanding your consciousness that success will come to you.

The first thing you must do becomes aware of your third eye. It is located in between your eyebrows, above your nose. It can take some time spent on meditation and practice even to reach this step.

To start, pick a day when you don't have anything planned or other obligations to worry about. The beginning of a weekend or a day off work is excellent. It would be best if you planned this initial moment out in advance. After this first time, running through the rest of what you have will be easier.

To start with, remember that what you are dealing with is a very subtle sort of perception. What you're feeling won't be anything too dramatic. It could be that you only start out feeling a faint tingling or pressure in the location of your third eye, but that's enough to begin what we're working on. Remember, you want things to come to you.

Some sort of vibration, hard to detect, is already there between the eyebrows in everybody. This exercise aims to show you how to notice vibration to allow it to blossom into the awakened power of the Third Eye.

Choose a quiet room where you can meditate uninterrupted for at least an hour. You don't have to be alone, but there should not be anyone in the room who is not participating in the ritual with you. It would be pretty counterintuitive if others interrupted you while you were meditating.

You want to be in a place where you can relax. Deep breathing and clearing your mind are great ways to get in the right place to explore the third eye for guidance on achieving this super-relaxed state.

To prepare the room, you'll want to light candles around the room. Then comes the time to make sure you have the proper attire. You'll want to take off your shoes and undo your belt, tie, or any other articles of clothing you have tied around you, along with your watch.

You'll want to close your eyes; they'll be closed until the end of the exercise. To begin with, you'll want to relax for 2 or 3 minutes. You'll want to be aware of your body and its energy. Focus on that for a while.

Then, you want to be aware without any particular concentration on any part of your body. Allow yourself to embrace the energy.

You now want to be aware of the area between your eyebrows. This is where you'll want to focus your attention since this is the location of the third eye. Counterintuitively, you don't want to concentrate too much. If you take hold of your Third Eye area with a too-tight focus, the process can't unfold. Instead, you want to see what happens spontaneously. If your breath becomes more intense, changing nature, you want to follow that and allow that to happen.

You want to remain 'just aware' of this place between your eyebrows, breathing deeply for about 5 minutes. However, it doesn't matter if you have the time exactly right or not, so there's no need to be exactly precise.

Next, place the palm of your hand in front of the area where your third eye chakra is located. Make sure that the handwriting doesn't touch the skin but hovers above. For a few minutes, stay in this position, lying on the floor with your eyes closed.

Next, you want to put your hand back by your side. Make sure to keep your eyes closed. Then, start looking for a vibration between your eyebrows, as mentioned before. It might feel a precise beat or a sense of tingling in several different ways. It could even feel like a somewhat blurry pressure, a heavy feeling between the eyebrows.

Again, you don't want to try too hard. Remember that it is impossible to force this experience. Take it slow, and wait for this vibration to build up. You want to relax and flow with what comes.

At this point, you want to be extremely still. You want to be able to feel the energy around you. It's easier for you to tune into higher states of consciousness when you're still.

This trick here is not focusing too much on your third eye. To achieve this state, you should observe without interaction. In this state of passive observation, you will begin to see with your third eye.

Remember, if any of this experience becomes too much for you at any point, you only have to open your eyes again, and the session will be over -- you'll instantly be restored to ordinary consciousness.

You'll have to work at this for a fair amount of time before you start envisioning the sort of sights that you might typically associate with opening the third eye. However, with each meditation session that you attempt to draw out the power of the third eye, you'll gain a deeper and deeper understanding of both yourself and the world around you.

Third Eye Visions

At this point, we'd best clear up some possible misconceptions about sight with the third eye. You don't see visions as a psychic would. What you are doing instead, what you are doing is expanding your company into new realms of consciousness. Psychics would feel an attachment to the pictures they see in their consciousness. When reaching visions of truth, however, you should be less interested in the specifics of what you see and focus on opening your mind's eye, allowing your state of consciousness to expand.

When this happens, you come to understand the higher matters of the universe, the completely different universe, a point where you find that you'll be unable to accurately describe what you have seen because the experience is beyond the tools of language we have for it. Many beginners and folks new to the craft expect to see an exciting new spiritual world with their physical sight and eyes. But this is fundamentally impossible because the part of your mind that processes the picture is the part that has been blinded. To see, you must step out of your mind. Again: To see, stop looking. Of course, this will take practice and patience.

One thing to remember is how you will perceive things once you open your third eye. This is a bit of a secret among those who already have this knowledge, one that can change how you approach opening your third eye.

In your everyday life, when you look at something, you look at the different parts of an image, after which what you see is processed by your conscious mind. This is what we usually think of as vision, stemming from the ordinary workings of your mind. However, this mental layer is the part of you preventing you from accessing the site that gives you access to spiritual worlds. You have to turn off this mental overlay over the image to see visions of the spiritual world, auras, and spiritual beings.

This is the secret you want to keep in mind; instead of looking at an image as the sum of its details, you want to focus on the very fact of seeing. Usually, your vision would be occupied by an object in front of you and finding out its particulars, which categories you can assign to the thing in your mind. Instead, you want to forget that you should know to look at the components of what you see and become aware of the higher concept of seeing. Again, to learn, you must stop looking.

Another thing to be aware of when attempting to see with your third eye is the color difference you will see. When looking into the higher plan, you won't see the light from the sun or know from any lamp. Instead, the objects and beings you encounter can be seen because they shed their light. Opening your third eye exposes you to a whole new world of color.

These figures will appear to you as 'made of colors' in an environment of partial darkness. However, it would help if you remembered that a world's astral colors are apart from the physical ones. Again we run into problems with the limitations of our language for describing mystical experiences. To represent these colors precisely is impossible due to the lack of counterpoints we can perceive in the material world. For example, you may find that astral colors may appear to you like a mix of differences. But when you try to mix the other components of a heavenly color, it won't seem to work, unlike colors in the material world.

You can mix blue and yellow in the material world and have green. However, you'll see something different when you open your eyes to the astral world. The colors in the astral world are instead made of many small and gleaming points. For example, you may see a 'blue-yellow-green' in which blue, yellow, and green issues are woven together. This variety and beauty are standard for astral colors, rarely uniform. It's impossible to compare these colors to anything we can observe in our physical reality.

As your third eye begins to develop, you may be able to behold more layers of this plan or even start to see multiple of these layers simultaneously. You may eventually reach a point in opening your third eye where you simultaneously see the physical and spiritual worlds in your vision.

This beauty is beyond anything you have experienced. It can become too much sometimes, to the point of being unbearable. Your life starts to become a constant wonder and great fun.

Here is something I recommend you keep in mind as you awaken your third eye; you'll probably find it more satisfying if you don't try to interpret many of the visions you experience. As you go about performing these exercises, you'll see a myriad of wondrous sights. It's best to accept that it will be a while before you fully comprehend what they mean. To safely interpret the images you see takes a great deal of experience. Don't let that stop you from trying if you wish, however!

Another thing you'll want to keep in mind is which world you see is the real one and the "fake" one. When people begin opening the third eye, they usually have preconceptions about what they see. They consider that the physical world they experience in their day-to-day lives is the "real one" and that the non-physical world is only an overlay of reality.

Though, both of these worlds are as real as the other. The only difference is how you perceive them. While you perceive the physical world with your mind, the spiritual world is perceived with your newly discovered third eye.

Not just colors or objects that may at some point visit know from you now, but actual beings of the astral plane. These can manifest as spiritual guides for you or angels, beings of a higher plane. Again, you want to ensure that you don't force communication with them. As with everything else with the third eye, it's best first to observe and analyze later.

Chakra Healing

Chapter 8. The Third Eye Chakra and Everyday Life: How to Nourish Your Third Eye

Awakening the third eye and healing the pineal gland is not the journey's end. It is an ongoing balancing, strengthening, and nurturing of the third eye chakra to keep it open and energized. Your improvement and attaining your highest self is a perpetual work in progress. This chapter will discuss various methods for controlling the third eye chakra healthy.

Thankfully, these methods and techniques can be easily incorporated into your lifestyle. The idea is that whichever of these methods you adopt should become habits that go hand in hand with meditation. The result will be a powerful and effective routine that allows you to nurture your excellent third eye continually.

Third Eye Chakra: Nourishing Foods

The third eye chakra is related to the spiritual rather than the physical realm. This may make you think that it is not influenced by your physical activities, namely, your food. Several specific "superfoods" can keep the third eye chakra balanced and unblocked. Eating a combination of these foods keeps your intuition strong and your perception open.

Additionally, the third eye resonates with beauty. Believe it or not, the way you arrange your food on your plate and integrate different colors can bring joy to your third eye. Luckily, the list of foods that promote third eye chakra health is long and varied, with something in it for everyone. You do not need to go on a restrictive diet or deprive yourself. Just make sure you eat as much of the following foods as you can:

1. Indigo, violet, and purple-colored foods are suitable for the pineal gland and, in turn, for the third eye chakra. They are also great for regulating blood pressure and powerful antioxidants that keep your brain performing at optimum health. These include:

- Eggplant.
- Purple grapes.
- Blueberries.
- Figs.
- Purple kale.
- Prunes.
- Plums.
- Purple onions.
- Raisins.
- Purple cabbage.
- Blackberries.

The color pigments in these foods represent dreams, inner thoughts, and inner harmony with the universe.

2. Dark chocolate enhances brain clarity and contains serotonin, a mood-boosting hormone. Try having a piece before you meditate to boost your focus and improve your enjoyment.

Go ahead and have as much dark chocolate as you want when you are in the process of awakening your third eye chakra.

Note: The keyword here is "dark" chocolate, not milk or white chocolate.

3. Nuts and seeds are powerful brain nutrients that help focus and clarity. Pumpkin seeds and almonds are specifically recommended.

4. Fish contains Omega-3 fatty acids, another great brain nutrient that enhances attention and concentration. Try to eat fish at least two times a week when you open your third eye and once a week after that.

5. Herbs and spices maintain nervous system health and enhance the senses. Poppy seeds, mugwort, juniper, rosemary, and mint are incredibly potent. Turmeric has been used since ancient times to promote overall brain health.

6. We all know we should drink plenty of water, but how many of us remember to drink enough throughout the day? It is essential to keep your body hydrated throughout the day to keep your mind clear and focused. Water is also the best way to help flush body toxins regularly. Always drink a glass of water before you meditate.

In general, a sensible, healthy diet containing plenty of fresh fruits, vegetables, and healthy fats will keep the whole chakra system open and balanced—and keep you in better health.

Physical Exercise and Nature

This is a no-brainer. A healthy body equals a healthy mind, which leads to a balanced chakra system. You may already be practicing some form of physical exercise or engaging in a specific sport, which is excellent.

Any form of exercise will keep the energy flowing and your chakras balanced. However, you may want to consider the following physical activities that are specifically in harmony with third eye health:

Dance. Dance heightens creativity and perception while also toning the body. Any dance form is beneficial for third eye health, including dance-style aerobics.

Gymnastics. Exercises that challenge your balance and coordination are excellent for balancing the chakras.

Yoga. Yoga is, by far, the best physical exercise for your third eye. This is because yoga movements and positions are specifically geared to open up the chakra system and allow a sustained energy flow between all of the chakras. It also promotes physical flexibility and tones the body. Consider taking a beginner's yoga class if this resonates with you.

Nature. Any exercise you can practice outdoors in your heart is lovely for third eye chakra health. Hiking, swimming, climbing, nature walks, and cycling is perfect for promoting physical and spiritual health. You will benefit from fresh air, the inner peace of communing with nature, and a good workout for your muscles.

Keep a Dream Journal

Having psychic dreams is one of the most significant signs that your third eye is open. When it awakens, it sends vibrations through your system that, for promoting, enable the physical body to separate from the act of dreaming, allowing the dreams to come straight from the third eye.

While some people can remember their dreams very vividly, others only remember vague details or can't remember their dreams at all.

However, the third eye awakening usually makes the dream experience more vivid, so you can expect to remember your dreams quite clearly.

Keeping a dream journal will allow you to monitor your dreams to recognize any meaningful messages or symbols. Reviewing the content and development of your dreams will also help you to separate average goals from psychic ones.

Normal vs. Psychic Dreams

Often, our dreams have no meaning. Psychic visions are when we are given clear messages about specific people or future events from our third eye. Look for the following in your plans:

● Things that hold strong symbolism or meaning for you. This is the third eye's way of alerting you that the goal is different.

● Psychic dreams are surprisingly vivid. You can recall every detail. The next time you have such a vivid dream, it could be a message from another realm.

This is why keeping a dream journal can be extremely helpful. It is a great way to review the progression of your dreams as your third eye chakra awakens. You will learn to recognize dream patterns and analyze goals that do not conform to how they may contain messages.

Keeping a dream journal requires a few minutes of your time each morning. Record any dreams you remember from the night before as soon as you wake up. Try to remember as many details as possible.

Promotingenable, write down any personal symbolism you feel is essential and what you think it means for each dream.

Record the date without an entry on days when you can't remember your dreams.

Every week or two, review your entries and look for patterns in your dreams, recurring symbols, and possible messages.

Indigo light

Indigo light is the light associated with the third eye chakra. It is also called Royal Blue. Indigo is the color of inner wisdom and deep knowing, allowing us to experience unique spiritual gifts.

We must turn to the night to nurture the third eye chakra with indigo light. A starlit or moonlit night is the best way to expose your whole body to this powerful color. Stargazing, moon-gazing, and meditating under the night sky are ideal ways to bask in the miraculous power of indigo light.

Using Third Eye Colors in Your Home

The color indigo combines two colors, violet and deep blue. Surrounding yourself with these colors in your home (and in your office or other personal space) will ensure that your third eye is constantly exposed to its associated colors and their healing vibrations at all times. This will keep the third eye chakra unblocked and healthy because, if you remember, it loves beauty and recognizes its associated colors as beautiful.

Incorporate indigo, purple, and blue hues into your home décor wherever you can. This could be in wall art, rugs, pillows, curtains, or bedspreads. If you naturally love these colors, you can even use them in furniture or as the colors of walls.

You can also incorporate indigo, dark blue, and purple into your wardrobe and wear jewelry that contains precious or semi-precious stones in these colors. Silver is the metal that resonates best with the third eye, so silver jewelry embedded with these stones is a good choice.

Consider Binaural Beats

Binaural beats are designed soundtracks that help your brain enter a specific wavelength state. It would help if you listened to them through headphones. The tracks are designed to send a particular tone or sound frequency to the right ear and a different style to the left ear.

The two tones help your brain settle into the desired wavelength. Your brain processes the two frequencies and then creates the binaural beat's third frequency.

Binaural beats boost brain focus, increase productivity, alleviate depression and anxiety, and promote better sleep quality. Research on this form of "sound therapy," if you will, is somewhat inconclusive.

However, you may want to give binaural beats a try. Users have reported better quality sleep and relief from stress and anxiety. Binaural beats can help promote third eye chakra energy by allowing the brain to vibrate at a calmer frequency. It is doubtful that binaural beats will be very beneficial, but combined with meditation and other techniques, they may be perfect for you.

The best way is to experiment with different frequencies and see what happens. Various tracks are available online and through binaural beat apps, which are inexpensive.

Aromatherapy

Essential oils are lovely on many levels. Skeptics see them as a kind of glorified perfume, but actually, science has confirmed their therapeutic properties through hundreds of studies. The olfactory nerves are directly connected to the brain,d when essential oils are inhaled, they're very quickly transmitted to the area, where their healing properties promptly take effect.

Essential oils have calming, energizing, and pain-relieving qualities that range from managing anxiety, alleviating depression, and promoting sleep, to increasing focus—among other things.

Certain essential oils are highly beneficial to the health of the third eye chakra. Their wonderful fragrances will cleanse, nurture, and balance while filling your home with a subtle scent that everybody will love. Try the following essential oils:

- Nutmeg.

- Sandalwood.

- Myrrh.

- Grapefruit.

- Lavender.

- Chamomile.

How to Use Essential Oils

- Essential oils can be used in a diffuser so that you inhale the scent.

● They can be used in a warm bath for a refreshing and relaxing experience.

● Try spraying bed linen with a light mist of essential oil so that you can inhale the fragrance as you sleep. You can also place a cotton ball soaked in a few drops of oil on your nightstand.

● Use essential oils during meditation for a more profound experience.

● Use a few drops on your inner elbows. Its fragrance will remain with you throughout most of the day.

● Put a drop of essential oil directly on your third eye chakra.

● You can combine two or three of the oils listed above for variety. Play around and see which ones resonate the most with your senses.

Note: always use a carrier oil when using essential oils directly on the skin, and be very careful that it doesn't get into your eyes.

Consider Yoga

We touched on yoga lightly in a previous section. Yoga is a vast realm consisting of various schools and practices.

However, if you wish to consider yoga as an additional subject, here are the basics you need to know:

● Yoga has been used since ancient times to heal, open, and balance the chakra system.

● There are specific yoga positions or "asanas" Specific yoga positions or "asanas" are used to open and unblock the third eye chakra. Most of these asanas can be practiced by beginners.

There are dozens of simple yoga techniques for beginners on YouTube: so instead of rushing out to sign up for a class, try practicing along with some of these videos. (Search for yoga postures designed to open the third eye chakra). If you feel that yoga is something you can get into, consider a beginner's class.

Use Crystals and Stones for Third Eye Chakra Healing

Crystals and stones contain vibrational energy that resonates with the various chakras. Use crystals and stones, rock colors associated with the third eye chakra, to enhance intuition and nurture your mind's eye with cleansing energy.

The following stones and crystals are recommended:

Amethyst. This precious gem has been used traditionally for healing the third eye chakra. It is also believed to enhance wisdom.

Sodalite. This dark blue stone stimulates the pineal gland and helps develop psychic gifts. It also promotes intuition and clarity.

Purple Fluorite. This is a semi-precious stone that promotes clarity of thought and increases intuition.

Indigo Kyanite. This stone contains powerful energy for the pineal gland and helps develop psychic gifts. It also works to balance and align the whole chakra system.

Black Obsidian. This beautiful crystal promotes the balance of the third eye chakra.

Lapis Lazuli. This beautiful stone is perfect to wear in jewelry, such as earrings or rings. It contains excellent healing properties for the third eye chakra and calms the mind.

Moldavite. This is a semi-precious stone with a dark green color. Although not directly related to the third eye chakra, its vibrational energy helps clear negative thoughts and cleanse all of the chakras.

Azurite. This is another blue stone that helps develop psychic abilities. It also helps promote deep meditative states and is good to hold in your hand or keep beside you when meditating.

Stones and crystals can be worn in jewelry or carried in your pocket or handbag, held in your hand, or placed directly on the third eye chakra during meditation.

You can purchase non-precious purple and indigo-colored crystals and place them in bowls around your home or office. Put them on your third eye chakra for a few minutes to enjoy their healing energy more profoundly, even when not meditating.

Practice Affirmations

Affirmations are statements you repeat to yourself to empower your mind and replace limiting beliefs with positive ones. They target any area of your life that you want to improve, such as self-confidence, food addictions, overthinking, and productivity, among other things. Likewise, positive affirmations can be used to heal, nurture, and empower the third eye chakra and expand your consciousness.

Affirmations work to rewire your brain. When repeated repeatedly, the brain learns to believe they are true. It creates neural pathways related to these affirmations, which it perceives as truths. The brain then acts upon those truths, changing your perception and behavior. This is a process called neuroplasticity, where your brain learns to enforce a particular belief and trigger your actions and emotions accordingly. Suffice it to say that affirmations are not a bogus fad but potent tools used in many fields of psychotherapy and various rehabilitation programs.

Affirmations have three basic rules that need to be followed:

● They should be stated out loud. Not necessarily in a loud voice. Whispering them to yourself is ok as long as they are physically uttered.

● They should be displayed with conviction.

● They should always be in the present tense (and sometimes in the future tense) but never in the past tense.

Some proponents stress that affirmations should be stated while standing in front of a mirror and looking yourself in the eye. However, this is not carved in stone and understandably may feel too awkward for some people. If you are new to affirmations, expect to feel more uncomfortable at first. Just stick to it, and you will soon learn to repeat them with purpose and complete conviction.

Chapter 9. The Biggest Mistakes People Make When Trying to Activate the Third Eye

If there is something worse than not doing something, it is incorrect. The same is true for third eye activation. If you try to awaken your third eye and do it poorly, you are up for bad experiences. Third eye awakening is a powerful practice that must be done carefully and with great dedication.

If you are looking for quick results or instant gratification, you will be stepping into the wrong realm. Some people keep trying but never really have any luck with their third eye activation. It isn't that the third eye is not present in them; they seem improperly looking for something. Not understanding or misinterpreting the signs can also lead to failure or desperation.

The following are some of the people's mistakes while activating their third eye. It would help if you avoided them.

Indulging in Misinformation

TV, media, and the internet are great tools for spreading misinformation. They have a knack for making a mountain of a molehill. They can make you believe absurd things that may lead to desperation in the end. Before you begin your third eye activation, you must make yourself aware of what you will encounter on your way. Do not expect too much or too little. Judging the gap always prevents falling into it. Do your homework properly before you embark on the journey of activating your third eye.

Lack of Trust

Trust is a significant factor when you go on any journey, especially involving adventure. Third eye activation is an adventure trip like you have never taken. To experience it, you must have trust in yourself and your instincts. It would help if you did not distrust anything you see or feel while activating your third eye. It would help if you also gave proper importance to the changes you experience on the way. Remaining conscious of even the smallest of events is very important.

Lack of Purpose

People without a clear purpose for activating their third eye will face failures. Activating the third eye is not a walk in the park. You can't shake it off as you do with other things. It starts some irreversible processes. It would help if you had a definite purpose for activating the third eye. Only then will you be able to judge the amount of success you have achieved in your pursuits. If you are not looking for something specific, you may not find anything.

Lack of Technique

Following a proper technique is very important for activating the third eye. Third eye activation may look like an undefined path. The journey inside doesn't have a definite route, but using the proper technique is very important, or you can start feeling lost. Pick a method that suits you the best, and please follow it carefully. Do not keep changing your plans, or you may not achieve anything. Remain regular in your practice and do it with great devotion. People who take this lightly end up wasting their time.

Trying too Hard

Do not try too hard. Those who want quick success often start trying too hard in the beginning. It may lead to desperation, your mind will begin cooking up false stories, and both will lead to failure. When activating your third eye, focus on the technique and let things happen independently. Do not try to force your mind to think in a particular way or imagine something. Overdependence on visualization will lead to framing false notions in your mind. You may start viewing items you want to see without achieving anything.

Stop Looking for the Wrong Signs

It would help if you looked for the right signs. Some so-called experts have attached wrong notions to the third eye activation method. They have made people believe that third eye activation will only happen if they get specific signs. This is inaccurate. Look for the subtle changes taking place inside you. Trust your instincts and take the lead. Do not go by the wrong notions. Your experience with third eye awakening may be different from others. If you keep looking for the affairs, you may never feel satisfied.

No Instant Results

Third eye activation is not similar to ordering anything on the internet. It doesn't happen instantaneously. Even after your third eye has awakened, you may not be able to see a significant change for a very long time. Honing your abilities takes much longer than that and requires much practice. You must pay great attention to this aspect.

Not Enough Practice

This is a continuation of the previous point. You will need to practice your skills for quite some time to have measurable results. Even if your third eye is active, it will not have significant consequences if you fail to practice it regularly. You have to train your mind to look in the right direction. Your mind must learn to recognize the signs. It must know to look at things with better insight. All this will only happen when you practice regularly. Make meditation a part of your schedule. Do not miss it or give excuses to yourself. By doing so, you'll only be bringing failure to your pursuit.

Avoid Overpublicizing Your Efforts

The journey to awakening your third eye is a personal quest. It is a long journey, and the ride is never smooth. You must avoid talking about it to your friends. Such discussions spark negative criticism and envy. You may start getting labeled or ridiculed, leading to doubts. Please keep it to yourself, and keep practicing. It is one of the best ways to preserve positive energy and get better results.

Five Myths about the Third Eye and Reasons the Media Wants You to Stay Asleep

It isn't uncommon for people to get wrong notions about things they don't understand quite clearly. In the past, people who understood the powers of the third eye rose to the upper ranks of society pretty fast. The third eye empowered them with more extraordinary intellect, wisdom, and foresight. The power to see better than others is a gift that can help you in many ways. People in power often want to stay in control and need people to dominate.

This is one of the reasons that society is so ignorant about the concept of the third eye. Evidence and symbolism clearly state that all civilizations and cultures knew about the third eye concept.

The pineal gland is similar to the shape of a pinecone. We see that ancient civilizations couldn't have had scientific knowledge about the pineal gland's importance in our bodies. However, they understood that this gland could do some amazing things. There is no other explanation for depictions of the pinecone as the third eye across all cultures.

Ancient Egyptians preserved the pineal gland separately during the mummification process. They wouldn't have gone to such lengths if they didn't understand its significance. Even their arts and artifacts have a clear depiction of the third eye. Egyptian civilization was thought to rely too much on mystical powers, and they achieved some excellent feats in their time.

Greek Gods are also shown carrying a pinecone in their depictions. Arts and artifacts of the time use this symbolism heavily.

The same goes for the Babylonians. Babylonian gods can be seen holding pinecones.

Eastern cultures also demonstrated that the secrets of the third eye were known to them. Both Hindu and Buddhist traditions show that they knew about the third eye. One of the most prominent Hindu traditions, Shiva, is depicted with a third physical eye. It is said that he can see the past, present, and future with this eye. Followers of this faith also believe that Lord Shiva can open this eye to nurture or destroy this world.

Buddhist culture treats the third eye with great reverence. It believes that the third eye is the source of higher consciousness. This culture has always given incredible importance to freedom from the cycle of birth and death. It believes that the primary goal of life is to achieve 'Nirvana,' i.e., release from the process of life. The Buddhist culture believes Nirvana can only be accomplished if you do not have 'Karma' that ties you to the world. They believe that higher consciousness can help them in achieving this state.

We see that most cultures have known about the third eye for years. Although they did not have any means of communication back then, their depictions and beliefs are similar. This means that some people across all these cultures knew the third eye.

The secret of the third eye has remained guarded among cultures because people who had unlocked the secret either didn't want this power to get into the wrong hands or liked all of the capacity for themselves. The third eye opens up the mind of the practitioner. Once your wisdom expands, you wouldn't remain a follower and instead become a leader. This might be one reason why the power of the third eye was kept a secret.

People in powerful places want others to follow them. This can only happen if the people in the lower strata struggle to survive. Our world runs on the mechanics of power. The people on the top often try to control power with their own hands. This is one main reason why education was restricted to the tutor class. Even the Holy Bible was written in a language ordinary people didn't understand. Only matters that helped keep them under control were fed to the people.

The same has been the case with the third eye. Influential people in the world knew about the powers of the third eye – and have been using them. But the secrets of the third eye were never revealed to the common masses. People only came to know what bits trickled from the top in the form of gossip. It is projected as a power that can cause great harm. It is also said that activating or controlling the third eye muscles is impossible for everyone.

Most of these beliefs do not have any merit. We will now discuss five myths about the third eye and their truth.

I.   Everyone cannot have the power of the Third Eye, which is closed in most of us. Only a chosen few can open it.

This is one of the biggest lies you could believe. The third eye is in everyone. The pineal gland is the physical location of this metaphysical eye. We all have it. It is a gland that performs several vital functions in your body. Without the pineal gland, you would be in a pretty sorry state. You would have no sense of happiness and erratic sleep and wake patterns. The pineal gland regulates your body's circadian rhythms and tells you about day and night. Our third eye is not entirely closed. We all have the power of intuition, which shows that the third eye functions in all of us, although not with great accuracy. So, the first part of the myth is baseless. We all have the physical gland necessary for the proper functioning of the third eye. You can activate the third eye and use its full potential. You do not need to be a particular individual or an incarnation to open an individual or image to open the third eye. Any individual who can devote some time and meditate can open the third eye.

The only thing required to open the third eye is dedication. You will have to follow the path of meditation and polish your powers. The pineal gland is present in all of us, but the power of higher consciousness, intuition, and foresight must be practiced. Meditation will enhance your ability to experience these powers. You can do this irrespective of class, race, or religion. The concept of the third eye is not religious but spiritual.

2.   It would help if you opened your third eye.

The third eye is inside you. If you want to open your third eye, you may not need anyone. If you make up your mind and start working in the right direction, the powers of the third eye will become vital to you. Teachers, people with already honed psychic abilities, and enlightened beings can help you on your path. However, if you believe that it is a power that someone can give you, then you are seriously mistaken. If someone has been telling you so, you are being misled.

You will undoubtedly need dedication and devotion to open your third eye, but you do not need others. If you want to open up your third eye, then learn how to do that and move ahead on the path.

3.   Some people can open their third eye instantaneously.

The third eye is not an implant that needs to be placed inside you. It is a physical gland that is already inside you. The psychic part of the third eye is inactive in most of us as we often do not use it. But that doesn't mean someone could flip a switch and open your third eye. It is your consciousness, and you need to cultivate it. You can easily extend your third eye if you give it proper attention.

It may take some time, and you may not experience anything exemplary initially. You first need to activate your third eye and then increase its powers. It is similar to pumping iron in the gym. The more you work on it, the better you get. A good teacher or coach can help you build the body faster but can't do the muscle building for you. Some people can activate their third eye in the first session, and others reach that point later. Nevertheless, anyone who wishes to open the third eye can do so.

4. The third eye is evil in nature.

No power is good or evil by nature. It is the way that energy is used that determines its character. The same goes for the third eye. You can develop several psychic abilities with the help of the third eye. If used in the right way, those psychic abilities can be helpful for people. However, they could be used to harm others or for nefarious motives. Such actions will have consequences for the initiator, too.

If one starts using the powers derived from the third eye for evil things, an accumulation of negative energies begins. It will have a substantial impact on your personality and thought process. You wouldn't remain the same person. Judicious use of such powers is essential.

5. It would help if you knew that your third eye is active.

There can be nothing further from the truth. The internet displays wrong notions that you will have specific experiences if your third eye awakens. This is like taming the untamable. The third eye opens the doors to another dimension. The possibilities are unlimited. Your experiences can vary considerably. You may not feel things like others have told you, yet you feel euphoric.

Actual third-eye experiences will vary from person to person. When your third eye opens, you will start feeling the differences in your thought process. Your mannerisms will start changing. Third eye opening will not mean that you'll instantaneously gain psychic powers. You may not feel anything different even after your third eye has awakened. It is only after regular practice that you start feeling the difference in your level of perception and awareness.

BONUS

DOWNLOAD YOUR FREE COPY OF REIKI HEALING

SCAN THE QR CODE AND GRAB YOUR FREE COPY NOW

Bonus 2: 7 Chakras healing music for meditative mind. Scan the QR

Conclusion

Everything begins with our health. Our well-being adds to our everyday outlook and emotional and physical health, whether in our personal or career lives. Reiki will add energy to create a more peaceful life, resulting in a happier, more productive life. The more you use the powerful force of Reiki, the more you will feel balanced!

The most significant benefit of Reiki healing treatment is that this treatment increases your energy power to help heal others and yourself quickly. By promoting relaxation, creating a peaceful feeling, and reducing stress, you will shift toward your unique spiritual, mental, and physical balance and experience your body's healing mechanisms starting to work more effectively.

Reiki is a non-invasive way to bring positive energy forces to create mind and body wellness. It is a fantastic feeling when this energy surrounds you and flows through your body and mind while you concentrate on health. It is a powerful tool that will change and improve your life while inspiring you to change and focus on a healthy body and mind.

Reiki's powerful and mystic force flows in and out of your physical body using crossings known as "chakras," feeding your organs and cells as they make their way through every part of your body and mind to keep you well.

When this force is interrupted or blocked, the affected areas can stop functioning and be detrimental to your health, which could cause illness or, even worse, a devastating disease. Reiki is a powerful way to prevent this blockage and help to keep that life force energy working to keep you healthy.

Your chakras are powerful energy centers that connect your entire being to the world around you. Understanding how their power works and caring for your mind, body, and soul in a way that puts your energy as a primary priority can help you harness their capabilities to improve how you navigate the world and the realms beyond what you perceive.

As the gateway leading to the realities beyond our perceivable world, the third eye is one of the most potent and accessible energy centers we can use to increase and improve the powers of the mind. This ganglion of energy heightens our brain's capacity and establishes a more vital link between what we can sense and how we understand the truths and realities we perceive.

Opening the third eye chakra is no simple task; it will take significant effort and time from your end. But as you tap into its powers, you will discover new perspectives and abilities that can eliminate much of the stress, anxiety, worry, and fear we tend to deal with in our day-to-day lives.

I hope this comprehensive guide has helped you understand what your third eye chakra can do for you and how you can reap its unique abilities. Always remember to heal your chakras and cleanse your spirit to minimize the risk of an overstimulated third eye and maximize the benefits of using the helpful capabilities that the Ajna chakra can give you access to.

Author's Note:

Dear reader,
Thank you for joining me in telling **Chakra Healing**.

I would appreciate a short review if you loved the book and have a minute to spare.
Your help in spreading the word is greatly appreciated.

Thank you!

Asana Swami
Richard Reikivic

LEAVE A REVIEW HERE-US

LEAVE A REVIEW HERE-UK

www.youbookseditions.com

Made in United States
Troutdale, OR
10/16/2023

13753761R00066